INNER LONDON EDUCATION AUTHORITY

EDUCATIONAL GYMNASTICS

A guide for Teachers

SIR WILLIAM HOUGHTON, *Education Officer*

THE COUNTY HALL · LONDON · S.E.1

First Edition	1962
Reprinted	1963
Second Reprint	1963
Third Reprint	1963
Fourth Reprint	1964
Fifth Reprint	1965
Sixth Reprint	1965
Seventh Reprint	1966
Eighth Reprint	1967
Ninth Reprint	1968
Tenth Reprint	1969
Eleventh Reprint	1969
Twelfth Reprint	1970
Thirteenth Reprint	1971
Fourteenth Reprint	1972

© Published by
THE INNER LONDON EDUCATION AUTHORITY
The County Hall, London, S.E.1
1972

Publication 7168 0291 0   **28p Postage extra**

FOREWORD

T HIS guide was compiled by the Authority's women inspectors of physical education primarily for the use of women teachers attending refresher courses organised by the Authority.

Repeated requests for copies have been received both from teachers in the Authority's service and from those outside. It has, therefore, been decided to print and publish the guide in book form. Copies are being distributed to primary and secondary schools where girls are taught. Teachers of boys' educational gymnastics may also find the guide helpful if they have attended an appropriate training or refresher course.

Courses in educational gymnastics based on this guide are organised at frequent intervals for teachers in the service of the Inner London Education Authority.

W. F. Houghton

Education Officer

CONTENTS

PAGE

CHAPTER I

INTRODUCTION TO EDUCATIONAL GYMNASTICS .. 1
The Plan of the Lesson 4

CHAPTER II

MOVEMENT THEMES 7
Movement Sequences 9

BASIC WORK FOR LOWER JUNIOR CHILDREN 10
Tasks for First and Second Year Children .. 11
Apparatus Work 16
Stages of development in Apparatus Work .. 17
Suggestions for tasks on the Cave Southampton
Apparatus 18

CHAPTER III

THEMES—Group I
I. Learning to Receive the Weight 23
Flight 27
II. Lifting and Lowering 29
III. Curling and Stretching 30
IV. Twisting 32
V. Shape 33
VI. Symmetry and Asymmetry 34
ADVANCED THEMES—Group II—For Secondary Girls
VII. Emphasis placed on selected parts of the
Body 36
VIII. Rhythm and Phrasing 37
IX. Circlings, Swingings and the use of Momen-
tum 39

X. Successive and Simultaneous Movement .. 41
XI. Parts of the Body leading the Movement .. 42
XII. Loss and Recovery of Balance 42

PARTNER AND GROUP WORK 43
Aspects of Work in Pairs 44
Aspects of Work in Threes 45

CHAPTER IV

THE FOUR MOVEMENT FACTORS 46
TIME 46
Time as a Theme 46
The use of Time with Movement Sequences and
Tasks 47

SPACE 47
Direction 47
The Path 47
Direction as a Theme 47
The use of Direction with Movement Sequences
and Tasks 47
Level.. 48
Level as a Theme 48
Use of Level with Movement Sequences and
Tasks 48

WEIGHT 48
Preparation—Action—Recovery 49
Accents 50

FLOW 51
Bound Flow 51
Free Flow 51
Combination of various Aspects of the Move-
ment Factors 52

CHAPTER V

PAGE

OBSERVATION 53

SAFETY PRECAUTIONS 54

Accommodation 54

Clothing 54

The Apparatus 54

THE USE AND ORGANISATION OF APPARATUS—

Use during the Introduction and Movement Training
section of the Lesson 55

Use in the climax of the Lesson 55

Progression in the Use of Apparatus 56

THE LIFTING OF APPARATUS 57

PROGRESSION 57

Elementary to Advanced Stages 57

DIAGRAM OF ANALYSIS OF MOVEMENT .. See end of book

CHAPTER I

INTRODUCTION TO EDUCATIONAL GYMNASTICS

This handbook has been compiled for use by teachers in the service of the Inner London Education Authority in an endeavour to clarify the present approach to the gymnastic lesson. We hope it will give advice and concrete help to those starting out with some uncertainty and trepidation upon this method of teaching until they have gained sufficient confidence and experience to branch out and enjoy to the full the opportunities which this work undoubtedly offers to all those with initiative and imagination.

Lessons are based on problems related to the management and control of the body with the teacher guiding the children through themes. These movement ideas have as their purpose the building up of a wide movement vocabulary from which the children learn to select the appropriate action for the task set. Each child is free to work out the problem individually within the limits set by the task which the teacher has chosen, and is expected to find a solution which makes real demands upon her, the repetition of which will be of value in training ' movement memory '. The teacher should observe carefully to see how they solve the different tasks, as some children may try to perform a favourite movement each time, which could produce a weakness such as the over-mobilisation of certain joints. In these cases the teacher should suggest to the children that different movements should be attempted.

Movement training, which gives an understanding of the theme, is done first on the floor in preparation for the work on the apparatus. As children attempt skills, whether accepted ones or those devised by themselves, the teacher must be ready to

1

give the technical advice which will help them to perform their skills competently and safely.

Suitable themes give constant stimulation to further inventiveness and demand increasing mental effort and concentration as the children work out solutions to the problems. There is a growing understanding and mastery of their bodies in movement and as confidence and sensitivity develop their movements become competent, fluent and skilful.

The training is based upon the work of Rudolf Laban who started his research over fifty years ago. He studied movement in all its forms—particularly in dance, drama, mime and in industry. He stressed the fact that each person possesses specific movement characteristics and a natural rhythm of moving which enables him or her to master some movements more easily than others. He showed that there is more to be considered than merely muscle and joints and to describe the factors essential to all movements he used the terms Time, Weight, Space and Flow. Careful observation of any action will confirm that these factors are always present, though blended in various ways. A new terminology has developed to express his theory in which ordinary words have taken on a specialised meaning.

The body is regarded as the agent or instrument of movement. If an instrument is to be well and fully used a knowledge of its parts and its potentialities is necessary. The child therefore should be made aware of one part of the body in relation to other parts or to the whole, and the term ' body awareness ' is associated with these experiences.

Movements of the human body can be functional, serving a practical purpose such as surmounting obstacles and handling objects or of an art form as in creative dance. Laban formulated certain concepts to provide for the analysis and development of movement. He defined the factors of movement as those of Weight, Space, Time and Flow.

The sensation received from a movement differs each time the emphasis placed on any one of these factors is altered. The movement potentialities of the body are used to the greatest advantage when the child can produce the appropriate blending of the Weight, Space, Time and Flow factors for any action.

2

WEIGHT

The term ' weight ' here covers not only the use made of the weight of the body but also the muscular action which together, enable the child to move with varying degrees of strength or lightness, as in touching, gripping, supporting or propelling. In heaviness there is an absence of ' light or strong ' tension, which is apparent when a child droops or ' lets go '.

SPACE

The Sphere of Movement

The body is surrounded by space into which, from a stationary base, it can extend in all directions and at all levels. This space is known as the body's ' Sphere of Movement '.

Within this sphere movements can be made:

  (i) away from or towards the centre of the body;
 (ii) in the space around the body moving neither inwards nor outwards;
(iii) with the limbs, near or far away from the body.

As a movement is made in space, the body can assume or move through a specific shape; the long extended, the small compact and round, the wide, or screw shape.

General Space

As soon as the body begins to travel, it moves into the general space. Here again movements can be made in different directions, forwards, backwards, sideways, upwards and downwards. High levels can be reached with stretches, leaps and bounds, and low levels by bending, curling up or rolling, on the floor.

TIME

Any movement uses a quantity of time: it may be quick, using little time, or slow, using much time. The speed of the movement or movement sequence need not be uniform throughout. Variations of speed may be developed into a rhythmic pattern. The quality of time is shown by suddenness or sustainment in movement.

FLOW

The flow of movement can be ' bound ' or ' free '. Any movement which can be stopped or held without difficulty at any stage

3

in the action is termed ' bound '. Any movement which is difficult to stop suddenly is termed ' free '. Because of the need to control the body in gymnastics ' bound ' flow is more often used. The nearest approach to ' free ' flow is in the continuity of action in movement sequences.

The present approach to physical education is aimed at helping the children to develop skill naturally and to understand the management and control of their bodies in movement. They are given the opportunity of using their own individual movement qualities and are introduced to a wider variation of the use of Time, Weight, Space and Flow. Those who are slow and strong or those who are quick and flexible are encouraged to make good use of these effort qualities. The teacher tries to draw ideas from and to help each child to use her own movement potentialities in solving the problems which are presented in the lesson. As the work develops, the children are encouraged to appreciate and experience efforts to which they are unaccustomed and to understand the value which these efforts have in helping them to master movement.

By starting with movements which the child is able to do and allowing her to continue within the limits of her own ability, she gains confidence so that she is ready and willing to attempt more difficult work. As children are creative, the material is presented in a way which stimulates inventiveness. The work is a constant challenge to the child both mentally and physically and she should be willing to accept this challenge. The teacher, in presenting movement problems, is appealing not only to the child's intelligence but also to her curiosity and sense of enjoyment and the child will experience great satisfaction in finding an answer to the task set. Active co-operation in the lesson may be gained more easily if there is an opportunity for every child to make a contribution in her own way (see diagram at back of book).

THE PLAN OF THE LESSON

1. Opening Activity (Limbering)

The children should be encouraged to start work immediately they enter the room. This work can take the form of:

(*a*) free practice of movements on any theme on which they have already worked,

or (*b*) simple tasks set by the teacher on the movement training used in the previous lesson.

2. Movement Training

In this section the main work on the chosen theme is carried out. The children work out freely the ideas which later they can apply to the apparatus. The theme selected will be determined by the needs of the class.

Tasks on a theme should be planned under the following three headings which may be arranged in any order:

A. For the whole body

In this part of the lesson the children learn to manage and control their bodies both with movements made on the spot and travelling over the floor.

B. With the weight supported on the arms

The aim of the early work should be to strengthen the arms and develop balancing skill. Until the children have both the strength and skill to balance on their hands the work will tend to remain on one spot. However, when they are sufficiently skilled, they can be asked to travel on their hands, keeping their feet off the floor, or, by continuous changes, from hands to feet to move about the room, delaying the arrival of their feet on the floor and so prolonging the balance.

C. Leg work

The emphasis here should be related to the propulsion of the body into the air and the reception of its weight on landing.

These three sections A, B and C should give the children good experience for situations which they will meet on the apparatus. Equal emphasis should be attached to all three aspects and while it may not be possible to cover them all in one lesson, the balance should be restored in subsequent ones.

3. Climax—Apparatus Work

In this section the movement experience of the earlier part of the lesson is applied to the apparatus. A task or tasks related to the theme should be set the apparatus arranged with imagination and variety and in such a way that the three parts of the movement training section are included if possible. Once confidence has been established in the use of apparatus and the children have become skilful in the management of their weight, flight on to, over and off apparatus should be encouraged.

Division of time within the lesson

The division of time within the lesson is dependent upon the number of periods each week and the facilities available. Where there are one or two gymnastic lessons a week in an equipped hall or gymnasium, at least half of each lesson should be devoted to the Climax. In the case of two gymnastic lessons a week in which apparatus is only available for one, lessons may be planned as follows:

LESSON 1—Work on the Opening Activity and Movement Training of the selected theme.

LESSON 2—Work on the Opening Activity and the Climax of the same theme. Three-quarters of this time should be given to the Climax.

CHAPTER II

MOVEMENT THEMES

Many teachers have attempted to work on themes, a theme being one movement idea studied and developed throughout the lesson. They have, however, found difficulty in wording the tasks on the theme which they wish to set the children. It is hoped that those set out below will act as examples. We wish to emphasise that it is not necessary to hold rigidly to these tasks. Indeed, whenever a teacher can create her own tasks or theme she should do so, for in this way movement ideas will grow. The work will be enriched if every teacher makes her own contribution and is not working on exactly the same tasks. The opportunities in variety and development which this kind of work offers are infinite and immensely stimulating to both teacher and child.

The themes which follow have been chosen because they give not only a wide variety of experience and a vocabulary of movement which should enable the children to meet any situation concerned with the management of their bodies, but also because they give the fundamental experiences necessary for the development of objective and purposeful work in the gymnasium. For the Climax of the lesson a variety of apparatus can be used, and as previously stated the tasks set should be related to the problems which have already been worked out on the floor. *Small apparatus can be used but only as obstacles which the children go over, under, round or through.*

Within each theme are suggestions for tasks which can be set for the children. These tasks follow the headings given in the Plan of the Lesson, and are divided into movements for the whole body, movements with weight on the arms and leg work.

7

In all cases tasks to be worked out in one place on the floor precede those in which the body travels.

Throughout the work the children will learn that their weight can be received, supported, balanced or transferred on different parts. It is this awareness of the use of different parts of the body which is the important factor in producing the variety of movement.

Because all children are working as individuals and therefore each performing a different movement on the apparatus 'catching' would be difficult and unreliable. It is therefore, necessary from the beginning to teach the children how to make relaxed landings and how to fall and roll safely. This training is essential for security and Theme I ' Learning to Receive the Weight ' is devoted to this most important aspect of the work. Tasks from this theme must therefore be taken first and pursued until a sufficiently high standard of skill is acquired to ensure that the tasks set on apparatus can be safely executed. The pieces of apparatus to be used, their arrangement and the nature of the problems set, will determine how many of the tasks in Theme I must be mastered before work from other themes can be introduced. Before more advanced stages are reached on the apparatus, more difficult tasks from Theme I must be mastered.

The order in which themes other than Theme I are introduced is a matter of choice, though it will be found that some of the later themes demand a considerable movement vocabulary and concentrated thought. For this reason they may prove of most use with the more able or older girls. The teacher may find that she covers thoroughly only a few of the easier tasks in the theme with which she starts before moving on to others, setting in each a comparable number of tasks. Then she may return to her original theme and will find that the tasks she took formerly can now be performed better as a result of the children's increased knowledge and skill. Having taken a few more tasks in this theme she may go on from theme to theme finding the same improvement, and in addition include one or two of the more difficult tasks. After tasks have been set, the class should be given adequate time to find various possible solutions. From these, the children will then be able to select certain suitable movements, which, when put together, will form a sequence. Repetition of this sequence should enable the children to achieve a high standard of performance.

MOVEMENT SEQUENCES

The term 'movement sequence' is applied to a composite movement built up, by joining together, in an appropriate way, several comparatively short or simple movements, or positions. Any 'movement sequence' thus formed must show continuity, one part leading naturally into the next and must have definite starting and finishing positions.

If several positions are to be joined together in a satisfactory sequence they must not be too stable. If there is no tendency to continue to move easily between these positions, a sequence which travels cannot be made, e.g. it sometimes happens that a child will choose to take up a position lying face downwards on the floor and then try to continue to move in the forward direction (which can only be done by dragging herself along) and breaks the continuous transference of weight. This, however, could have been achieved if she had changed direction and rolled over sideways.

Movement sequences from the tasks given under the movement training sections of most themes can be developed by combining together several positions or movements under:

(i) A Whole body
(ii) B Weight supported on the arms
(iii) C Leg work
(iv) A, B and C
(v) A and B
(vi) B and C
(vii) A and C.

When the children understand the basic idea of the theme and what they are trying to do, they should be encouraged, where appropriate, to add to the interest and skill of their work by the use of variations in level, direction or time, when working on tasks and sequences.

9

The making up and perfecting of a sequence has great value because:

1. It trains movement memory.
2. It increases fluency of movement.
3. It serves as a testing time for the teacher in which to observe the needs of the class.
4. It demands a finished piece of work of a high standard.

To make the presentation of the work easier for teachers the tasks have been worded as they might be presented to the class. When reading the themes, it may appear that many tasks demand the same type of movement from the children. This is inevitable as all movement is limited by the structure of the body. The purpose of a theme is to highlight a particular way of moving and to increase the children's understanding and movement vocabulary. By emphasising the idea in the theme and in using the same terms of reference throughout, a particular aspect of movement becomes clarified in the minds of the children.

BASIC WORK FOR LOWER JUNIOR CHILDREN

The standard of work and knowledge of the children on entering the Junior School may be varied. The first task for the teacher is to assess the ability and knowledge of her class and to decide on its needs. She can reasonably expect that the majority of children will be accustomed to using agility apparatus and will have a general elementary knowledge of movement ideas.

In the Infant School the children have a natural inclination to climbing activities and to those in which they use hands and feet. The policy in the first years of the Junior School should be to concentrate afresh on the management of weight, training the children to land safely from many different situations, as they will be using higher and more demanding apparatus. They should be encouraged to use flight* increasingly and in varied ways in the activities they pursue.

In order to link the work of these lower classes with that of the Infant School, it is suggested that a large variety of work, all based on transferring the weight, should be given before taking

---

*Flight and the variations which can be used are described on page 27.

the children on to the more concentrated work which is involved in a lesson based on a single theme.

Children of this age can only manage to accomplish the tasks on a theme by holding stationary positions. They enjoy this but find great difficulty in joining them together into a skilful and logical sequence. Much of the spontaneity of their work is lost if they are urged too soon to concentrate on work on a single movement idea and to begin at too early an age to build up sequences.

For this reason it is advisable to let them have plenty of experience in transferring their weight. Variety and valuable experience comes from training in the various ways of using the feet in a jump and landing and in the use of the hands and feet in springing and weight bearing. Changes of speed, direction and working at different levels can help to develop the movement. The children can make use of these ideas not only on the floor but on the apparatus either in its free use or in action tasks.

TASKS FOR FIRST AND SECOND YEAR CHILDREN

A.—Whole body

TASK 1—Curl up small, tuck in your elbows, knees, hands, feet and head and try to travel softly and lightly over the floor. You may start with any part of your body on the floor but try to keep your head to your knees and remain tucked and small as you roll.

TASK 2—From standing put one part of the body (not the head) very low to the ground then take the weight on to this part; begin to close up and continue to move along the ground by rolling until you can transfer your weight on to your feet again and then jump up. Find all the different ways you can go down by putting a different part down first each time. Try to go down softly and carefully.

(The children will find that they can go down with knees, seat or side of one hip touching first; by bending low and twisting they can roll softly on to the back, or make one shoulder touch first.)

TASK 3—Walk slowly about the room, lower your body on

11

to the ground, curling and tucking as you go down, and continue to move by rolling tucked up until the weight is transferred on to the feet again.

Task 4—Run about the room, gradually slow down and lower your body on to the floor and continue to move by rolling tucked up. (Remind the children of the practice they did from standing in Task 1 and encourage them to use the safer parts of the body to touch the floor first, e.g. the seat and rounded back, the rounded shoulder.) Those children who can manage it may try to do this with a run and jump followed by a roll.

Task 5—Travel about the room by taking your weight from one part of your body to another. Do not keep your weight on the same parts while you move, try to keep changing so that different parts of your body take your weight.

Task 6—Travel about the room, taking your weight on different parts of your body and bring in changes of direction as you move.

Task 7—Travel about the room, taking your weight on different parts of your body and try to change the level at which you move, sometimes keep your movement low and close to the floor, sometimes high in the air.

Task 8—Move about the room, taking your weight on to different parts and as you do this try to change the speed at which you move. Make some parts of your movement very quick and sudden and some parts very slow.

Task 9—Move about the room, taking your weight on to different parts and be prepared on a signal, even when moving fast, to stop and hold your position instantaneously (' freezing ') and remain so until the signal is given to continue moving.

Task 10—Move about the room, taking your weight on to different parts of your body and as you do this think about the shape your body is making. Can you make it small and rounded and then change to a long narrow shape and then to a wide shape?

Task 11—Move about the room, taking your weight on to different parts of your body by twisting and turning in different ways; then move without any twisting. Try using a twist and move on without a twist and so on.

TASK 12—Can you move about the room, taking your weight on different parts of your body, but think about keeping your hands and feet close together sometimes, and far apart at other times?

TASK 13—Can you move about the room, taking your weight on different parts of your body, think of all the different things you can do with your legs while you are moving? Your feet can be close together or far apart, your legs can make patterns by being exactly the same or one leg can be bent and one straight, etc.

TASK 14—Moving about the room and taking your weight on different parts, think how much of the space around you you are using. Sometimes make your body, legs and arms stretch out in different ways so that you are using as much space as possible, and then change and make yourself small so that you take up very little space.

TASK 15—As above but with changes of speed, i.e. the spreading and stretching movement can be done quickly or slowly and so can the curling up movement.

B.—Weight supported on the arms

The weight bearing on the arms is an important part of the movement training as it is used in much of the apparatus work. It is, however, of value to give work which demands movement on the hands and feet for the following reasons:

(i) Particularly in vaulting, when flight is used, the weight of the body is often transferred between the hands and feet only and both hands and feet are often used simultaneously during the transfer of the weight wholly on to the arms or the feet.

(ii) Weight bearing on the arms demands considerable strength in the shoulder girdle and movements with the weight on the hands and feet can be used to develop the strength necessary to accomplish this feat satisfactorily.

The following suggestions for tasks where the weight is taken on the hands and feet may precede the stronger work in which the weight is supported on the arms only.

TASK 1—Travel about the room, using your hands and feet

13

only. Try to take your weight carefully both on to your hands and your feet.

TASK 2—Travel about the room on your hands and feet only, always moving both hands at the same time and then both feet at the same time.

TASK 3—Travel about the room using one hand and two feet. Use each hand but not at the same time.

TASK 4—Travel about the room, transferring your weight from your feet to your hands with a spring.

> *N.B.—This is a difficult technique to teach. The whole body should be clear of the floor after the spring from the feet, on landing the weight should be received through the arms with the fingers touching first, then the palm, followed by the heel of the hand and with a give in the elbow. The whole action of the arms is comparable with the reception of the weight by the legs after a jump. The action of the hands is similar to that of the feet and of the elbows to that of the knees.*

TASK 5—Travel about the room in different ways on your hands and feet and as you move try to make it more interesting by changing direction. Use a pushing movement with either your hands or feet; see if you can go sideways and backwards as well as forwards.

TASK 6—Travel about the room on your hands and feet, curling and stretching as you go. Make use of the stretch in particular to help you to get over the ground.

TASK 7—Travel about the room on your hands and feet and try to twist so that your feet, instead of following your hands, come down in a different place. Do this with your weight on one or two hands.

TASK 8—Travel about the room on your hands and feet, turning as you go, so that first your back will be to the ceiling and then your front. Later, kick up your leg as you turn over and take a little more weight on your arms.

Some of these tasks can be performed over canes and hoops, either placed on the floor or held by a partner. Suggestions are now given in which the weight is taken on the arms only.

Safety Precautions. When children are first attempting to take their weight on their arms they should be reminded constantly that:

(i) they should, without swinging their arms *place* their hands on the ground with fingers pointing forwards in line with their shoulders;

(ii) they should lift their heads by shortening the back of the neck and pushing the chin out.

TASK 9—Place your hands on the floor and, keeping them there try to lift the rest of your body off the floor, come down softly. If the feet are brought fairly close to the hands on landing and the head is lifted, it will be easier for the children to land softly. To guard against over balancing, the children should be encouraged, with a slight twist of the hips, to bring the feet down to the side as they land so that they are making a small turn. Make sure that the children do this movement to both sides.

TASK 10—As in Task 9, taking your weight on your arms, but recover to standing each time with a quick resilient jump.

TASK 11—As in Task 10, but when your feet have landed sometimes try to roll and jump up.

The children can now go on to tasks which ask for seat or feet high while balanced on their hands. They can also try to make the rounded, wide or narrow shapes. When they do this they can recover from the hand balance with or without a roll.

LEG WORK

TASK 1—Run, leap in the air, lift your chest and the top of your head high.

TASK 2—Run, jump high in the air and land on two feet, when you land bend your knees and try to let your seat touch your heels, but keep your back straight and your head up. From this low position twist and roll sideways on the floor, then jump up.

TASK 3—As above, but after landing jump up without a roll.

TASK 4—Run and jump, take off with a spring from two feet and land on both feet. Do this sometimes with a roll after landing and sometimes without a roll.

TASK 5—Run and jump, take off with one foot and land on two feet.

Task 6—Find different ways of taking off and landing with one or two feet.

Task 7—Run, jump in the air, and stretch your body, legs and arms, taking up as much space as possible. Your legs and arms can be in many different positions when you stretch. Can you find different ways of stretching?

Task 8—Use the idea of stretching but try it with a spring off one foot and then later off two feet. Try also landing sometimes with one foot after the other or with two feet together.

Task 9—Run, jump in the air and curl up, using as little space as possible, but always keep your head up. Can you find different positions in the air, using little space?

Task 10—Run, jump in the air and make a shape with your legs in front of you. How many different positions can you find with your legs in front? Try springing off two feet and off one, and also landing with one foot after the other, or on two feet.

Task 11—Run, jump and lift your legs to the side or behind you. Find how many different shapes you can make in the air by lifting your legs in different ways, bent or stretched, to the side or behind you.

Task 12—Run, jump and when you are in the air make a shape with your feet together. Find how many different shapes you can make with your feet together.

Task 13—As above, but with feet apart.

Any of these jumps can be done over a cane or a hoop placed on the floor or over a gap made by two canes or a hoop. They can also be used over canes or hoops held at different levels by a partner.

Apparatus Work

This is the climax of the lesson, and in these early stages the children should be confronted with many different settings of apparatus. They should be encouraged to utilize these obstacles in a lively and inventive way. Approaching the apparatus from different angles, they can use different parts of their body to support them when they climb on or let themselves down, and they can find the different shapes and directions which they can use in jumping on and off.

Tasks set for apparatus work can be of two types:

(a) 'The Action Task.' This has certain requirements which the children must fulfil when using the apparatus. It demands either:

    (i) that they follow a given path, which may be over and under certain parts, or it may demand the crossing of certain gaps;

or (ii) that the children arrive on or leave the apparatus transferring their weight according to certain conditions set by the teacher, e.g. arrive on a box or platform with the feet touching first, come off by taking your weight *on the box or platform* with your hands (it should be made clear that they never jump from a height on to the floor with their hands first, they must use their hands on the box and land on their feet on the floor).

(b) 'A Movement Task,' requires the children to use specific movement ideas while travelling on the apparatus. It is related to the lesson theme and demands an understanding and feeling for movement which is more suited to the older children, e.g. use a curling and stretching movement while travelling.

The action task is the more objective and suitable for younger children. The achievement of the task gives immediate and obvious satisfaction. The child, by concentrating on finding various ways of getting from A to B, and later, by adding changes of speed, level and direction, will gain experience and confidence which will be invaluable to her in all her later work.

Stages of development in Apparatus Work

1. Free use of the apparatus, also free use with continuous movement.

2. Finding different ways in which to support and suspend the body on different parts of the apparatus.

3. Getting on to each part of the apparatus in different ways, and coming down from these in different ways.

4. Action tasks to encourage continuous movement from piece to piece of the apparatus.

5. Use the first simple ideas from other themes on the apparatus. On the climbing apparatus at first this may be positional work. The children will find the various positions or shapes demanded by the theme and discover where on the apparatus they can take these positions and, in doing this, make use of their earlier experience by using different parts of the body to support or suspend them.

6. Use the action tasks, and begin to lead up to movement tasks, which will be taken in the themes by encouraging the children to bring into their movement at any stage the appropriate shape or action, such as curl, stretch, twist, which they have used in their floor work.

Once they can transfer their weight with safety, both on the floor and on apparatus, meet the challenge of varying arrangements and tasks, land with control or transmit the momentum of landing into a safe roll then undoubtedly they will be making progress. The progress will be, not only in body management, but in confidence, thoughtfulness and initiative.

SUGGESTIONS FOR TASKS ON THE APPARATUS

Cave Southampton Apparatus

Panels flat against the wall.

(Make sure the panels are hooked at the top.)

1. Run and leap on to the panel, spring off.

2. As above, but leap off one foot from the floor on to the other on the panel.

3. As above, but jump off two feet from the floor on to two feet on the panel.

4. Run, leap on to the panel and spring off with a twist in the air.

5. Run and leap on to the panel and using rope and panel to support you move up and down the panel, or make different shapes and then let yourself down to the floor with a part of your body other than your feet touching the ground first. Continue into a roll along the floor before you jump up.

Using the Outside Panels of the Bays

1. Free use of the panel—try to move continuously and avoid touching anyone else.
2. Use the floor and the panel, find different ways of climbing or jumping up and of coming off.
3. Jump on to the panel and in coming off find different ways of letting yourself down so that different parts of the body touch the floor first.
4. Use the hands and feet only, both on the floor and on the panel.
5. Use hands and feet on the panel and travel on other parts of the body on the floor.
6. Find different places where the body can be curled and different parts of the body to support or suspend you.
7. Find different places where the body can be stretched and different parts of the body to support or suspend you.
8. Find different places where the feet can be held higher than any other part of the body and different parts of the body to support or suspend you.
9. Find all sorts of balance positions in which only small parts of you touch the apparatus. Find some positions in which you use only one part of the apparatus and others in which you are using several parts of it, i.e. a heel in the panel, a hand on a rope and the other hand on a bar.

Using the Outside Panel of the Bay with a Form hooked on and a Mat placed beside the Form

1. Travel up the form on to the panel and come off on to the mat. Find ways of moving on the form using different parts of the body to support you; also find different ways of coming off.
2. Jump on to the form and find different ways of climbing or letting yourself down on to the mat.
3. Climb on to the form and find different ways of jumping off.
4. Move on the form and the panel and bring in changes of direction as you travel.
5. From an oblique run, cross the form with a strong thrust from one or two feet to land on the mat on the opposite side of the form.

6. As above but show a clear body shape in the air.

7. As 5 but turn in the air before landing.

8. From an oblique run, cross the form from a single or double take off from the floor, take the weight on one or two hands on the form and land on the mat on the opposite side of the form.

9. As 8 but show a clear body shape in the air.

10. As 8 but turn in the air before landing.

11. On landing from any task from 5-10 lead immediately into a movement taking you on to the panel, then either letting the body down to the floor or springing off the panel continue into a roll on the mat.

12. Movements making use of the underside of the form.

Using the Outside Panel of the Bays with a Form set parallel to the Panel. A Mat placed on the floor beside one half of the Form.

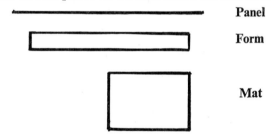

Panel

Form

Mat

1. Move from the floor on to the form then on to the panel. Come off using the form and/or the mat. Find how many different ways you can get up and come down from the panel.

2. Move from the floor to the panel and off again. Use changes of direction as you move.

3. As you move on this apparatus find different places where your body can be curled.

4. As above, finding different places and different ways of stretching the body.

Using the Cave Southampton Bay, two Beams and Ropes.

1. Travel from the ropes on to the first beam, continue to move on, over or under the next beam and return to the starting

place. Find as many different ways as you can of travelling across this apparatus.

2. Using the apparatus as above, find as many ways as you can of coming off the second beam.

Tasks of the type of 1 and 2 can also be carried out without the ropes and, by reversing the path of the movement, quite a different challenge may be presented.

Other arrangements of the Beams.

(i) First beam hip height, second beam head height.
(ii) Both beams the same height.
(iii) Both beams stretch height and on the back two uprights of the panel.
(iv) Using three beams in one bay.
    (a) First beam hip, second head and third stretch height.
    (b) First beam hip, second head and third hip height.
    (c) First beam hip, second and third head height.
(v) With two beams, one above the other at various heights and distances apart.
(vi) With three beams, two as in 5 and one either in front or behind the other two.
(vii) Forms can be inclined on to the beams or on to the inside of the panels.

Travelling from one side of the Bay to the other.

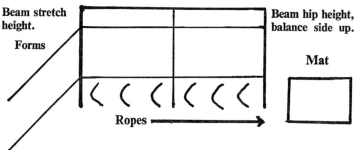

Beam stretch height.

Forms

Beam hip height, balance side up.

Mat

Ropes

Arrange a path of movement which goes from one side of the apparatus to the other. Let the children try to get from one side to the other without touching the ground. Arrange

21

alternative routes so that they can decide what they can manage, for instance:

COURSE A—Run and jump into a hoop and out of hoop on to panel—climb up and through panel to the other side—travel from rope to rope to the next panel—up and over or through the panel to the other side—travel from rope to rope to the third panel—climb up and over or up and through to the other side—jump off the panel on to the mat, roll across the mat to finish.

COURSE B—Start at the bottom of the form—travel up the underside of the form to the panel up and through or over the panel to the other side—along the top of the first beam up and over or through the second panel—travel under the second beam to the third panel—up and over or through the third panel and come off on to the floor with a part of your body other than your feet touching the ground first.

COURSE C—Start at the bottom of the form—travel up on top of the form to the panel—up and over or through the panel to the other side—travel along the first beam in any way to the second panel—climb up and over or through the third panel to the other side—travel along the second beam (flat side up) using your feet, or hands and feet only to support you to the third panel—climb up and over or through the third panel and find an interesting way of coming down to the ground.

N.B.—On no account should the travelling of these courses be taken as a race. This method tends to create queues and for this reason groups must be small.

The Bar Box

The bar box can be used in conjunction with the Cave Southampton apparatus in various ways. More usually, however, it is used together with form and/or mats to make interesting arrangement of obstacles.

CHAPTER III

GROUP I

THEME I
LEARNING TO RECEIVE AND TRANSFER THE WEIGHT

A teacher taking children in the upper part of the Junior School to whom this type of work is unfamiliar, should first use selected tasks from the Lower Junior section before embarking on this theme.

Children in the upper part of the Junior School who have worked through the Lower Junior section should be competent in the management of their weight and therefore it should not be necessary to spend long on this theme. It will in fact be noted, that tasks 1-4 are identical with those in the Lower Junior section. In some cases these children may be asked to tackle a few of the more difficult tasks in this theme and then move on to another.

In the Secondary School much the same holds good. Girls new to this work must start on Theme I and the ability of other classes must be assessed by the teacher before she decides what next to teach them.

She can assess their ability by taking one or two easier tasks from this theme and follow immediately with more difficult ones if they are well done. Should these tasks also be well performed she may decide to work on another theme.

It is essential to start with this theme as it is protective and teaches the safety precaution of ' tucking ' and rolling should the child fall or over-balance when landing. When the children are experimenting the teacher should help them to be aware of those parts of the body which are the most suitable for receiving their weights safely.

A—The whole body

From standing the children can learn to go down on to the floor with relaxation and softness in a variety of ways. In sinking to the floor in this manner they do not actively put themselves down, but allow the pull of gravity, which is always acting on the body, to take effect. Certain muscle-groups are acting as a ' brake ' on the speed with which the body is drawn to the ground. The ability to sink to the ground by ' putting the brake on ' instead of contracting the muscles or putting oneself down gives the type of movement required for safe landings. When children are landing from apparatus or from a jump they will meet the ground with some degree of force and it is essential to spread this force of impact in order to avoid injury to the spine and limbs. The force will be dispersed if there is sufficient ' give ' in the joints and if the movement continues in the direction of the impetus until control can be gained and balance recovered. Therefore always encourage the children to land on their feet with a deep ' give ' of the knees and hips. Where appropriate the ' give ' should be such that *the seat comes low and close to the heels*. Should they over-balance there must be a ' give ' in their arms as they throw them out to save themselves and they should tuck and continue rolling until they can regain control. If a forward landing is made and the balance lost, it is possible with a slight twist of the body, a *lowering of the hips* and a quick tuck, to roll sideways or to twist further and with the hips low put the seat down and roll backwards, still travelling in the direction of the impetus. In such cases provided that the hips are really low and the body tucked, the arms need not be used and can be held in. In order that the children may be prepared for such emergencies tasks A2, 3 and 4, and B3, C1 and 3 have been set. Throughout the themes it is advisable to add this tucking and rolling after landing until it becomes a protective habit.

Task 1—Curl up small, tuck in your elbows, knees, hands and feet and try to travel softly and lightly over the floor. You may start with any part of your body touching the floor but try to keep your head to your knees and remain tucked and small as you roll. (The children will find that they can go down with knees, seat or side of one hip touching first; by bending low and twisting they can roll softly on to the back or make one shoulder touch first.)

TASK 2—From standing get a part of the body very low to the ground then transfer the weight on to this part, begin to close up and continue to move along the ground by rolling until the weight is transferred on to the feet again and then jump up.

TASK 3—Walk slowly about the room, lower your body on to the ground curling and tucking up as you go down and continue to move by rolling tucked up until the weight is transferred on to the feet again.

TASK 4—Run about the room, gradually slow down and lower your body on to the floor and continue to move by rolling tucked up. (Let the children think of the practice they did from standing, i.e., Task 2, and encourage them to use the safer parts of the body to touch the floor first, e.g. seat, the rounded back, the rounded shoulder.) Those children who can manage it may try to do this with a run and jump.

TASK 5—Find the different part(s) of your body on which you can balance. (A balanced position is a stable one and its maintenance becomes increasingly difficult (a) when the area of the part of the body supporting the weight is reduced, (b) when the point or points of support are narrow or in a straight line. Teachers should observe carefully whether the children have taken up positions which require effort to maintain.)

TASK 6—Choose several different parts of your body on which you know you can hold a position and, using these parts one after the other, make a sequence moving easily from one position to the next, e.g. if the child chooses her knee, shoulders and one foot as points of balance she will show the starting position on the knee. She may then over-balance carefully and receive her weight on one hip, roll softly on to her shoulders, extending her feet high and balance—roll easily backwards or forwards until she can place one foot on the floor and balance on the one foot.

TASK 7—In this task the children should be asked to repeat the sequence they made up for Task 6, but move continuously, receiving their weight softly and smoothly on to each part in turn, passing through but not holding the positions.

TASK 8—Choose two parts of your body which are close to each other and rock from one to the other.

TASK 9—As Task 8 but after two or three rocks of increasing momentum continue into a roll and without pause continue rocking on the same parts.

TASK 10—As Task 9 but a roll or twist should take the body into position to rock between two other parts.

Practices of Tasks 8–10 should be taken for a short time only on the floor, and developed further in the group work, when mats should be used.

B—Weight supported on the arms

Safety—Precautions When children are first attempting to take their weight on their arms they should constantly be reminded that:

(i) they should without swinging their arms *place* their hands on the ground with fingers pointing forwards in line with their shoulders;

(ii) they should lift their heads by shortening the back of the neck and pushing the chin out.

TASK 1—Place your hands on the floor and, keeping them there, try to lift the rest of your body off the floor, come down softly. If the feet are brought fairly close to the hands on landing and the head is lifted, it will be easier for the children to land softly. To guard against over-balancing the children should be encouraged, with a slight twist of the hips, to bring the feet down to the side as they land, so that they are making a small turn. Make sure that the children do this movement to both sides.

TASK 2—As in Task 1, taking your weight on your arms, but recover to standing each time with a quick resilient jump.

TASK 3—As in Task 1, but when your feet have landed sometimes try to roll and jump up.

C—Leg work

TASK 1—Landing practice—run and leap in the air, land on two feet and recover to standing with a quick springy jump. If you over-balance, try to tuck up and roll.

Task 2—Run, leap and land with one foot after the other and continue running.

Task 3—Run, leap and turn in the air so that a landing is made facing another way. If you over-balance curl up and roll.

Coaching at first should be given throughout on relaxation, that is to say the deep ' giving ' of the legs so that the seat touches the heels with the back upright and the head erect. Once, however, the children are able to do this really competently their attention must be drawn to the place in which this type of landing is to be used, i.e. at the end of a movement or prior to a roll. When in a sequence they land and continue into another movement this should be in the nature of a rebound: the landing becoming the resilient preparation for the next movement. Instead of being dissipated the force of the landing is utilised to help the muscular action of the legs in thrusting the body into the air.

The children now have been given an opportunity to learn how to roll and protect themselves when they over-balance in three situations: (a) from standing, (b) when the weight is supported on the arms, and (c) from flight.

Sequences which combine A, B and/or C in any order may be used.

FLIGHT

Before leaving Theme I the children should be able to receive their weight with safety and to have understood the ways in which the force of landing can be absorbed. Work should now be given in every lesson which encourages them to propel their bodies into the air in flight. This is mainly achieved by a thrust from the arms and/or legs used in any of the following ways:

Using the feet only:

   (i) Taking off from one foot and landing on the other foot.
  (ii) Taking off from one foot and landing on the same foot.
 (iii) Taking off from one foot and landing on two feet.
 (iv) Taking off from two feet and landing on two feet.
  (v) Taking off from two feet and landing on one foot.

Using the hands and feet:
  (i) Taking off from one foot on to two hands and landing on one foot or two feet.
 (ii) Taking off from two feet on to two hands and landing on to one foot or two feet.
(iii) Taking off from one foot on to one hand and landing on one foot or two feet.
 (iv) Taking off from two feet on to one hand and landing on one foot or two feet.
  (v) Taking off from one foot on to one hand and then on to the other and landing on one foot or two feet.
 (vi) Taking off from two feet on to one hand and then on to the other and landing on one foot or two feet.

The above list gives all the various ways in which the use of the hands and feet can be combined. With her class, the teacher may take a movement using one of these ways and discuss with the children how they were used and then ask them to find other ways for themselves. On asking the children the alternative ways they have found, most methods will have been discovered. It is then valuable to be more specific and confine their choice, and to work on one or two of these ways only.

Interesting rhythms can be developed when using these ideas along or on and off forms.

Apart from the variety of work on the arms and legs, flight, when used on apparatus, will vary according to the objective:
  1. Finding different ways of climbing or getting on to a piece of apparatus and leaping off.
  2. Flight or leaping on to a piece of apparatus and coming down without a jump.
  3. Flight on to and off a piece of apparatus, the arrival on the apparatus, followed by an immediate take off.
  4. Flight over an obstacle.
  5. Flight off a moving piece of apparatus.
  6. Flight on to a moving piece of apparatus (e.g. a swinging climbing rope).

Numbers 4, 5 and 6 should not be set as tasks and used only when the children have become skilful. Flight over a fixed obstacle is a real hazard and jumping over such a piece of apparatus should be allowed only at the discretion of the teacher and according to the skill and ability of the children.

As the children increase their skill and experience a condition with regard to the feet and/or hands can be added to suitable tasks in any theme.

THEME II
LIFTING AND LOWERING

A. The whole body

TASK 1—Lift one part of the body high, come down softly, support your weight in a different way, then lift the same part high again. (The feet can be lifted high with the back or shoulders on the floor, or with just the hands as the point of support.)

TASK 2—Choose a starting position then lift one part of the body high, come down softly, support your weight in a different way and lift another part high.

TASK 3—Choose a starting position then lift one part of your body high and find a way of coming down softly so that this part of your body receives your weight first. (e.g. If the child has her weight on two hands and two feet and has lifted her seat high, she will find that by twisting her body she can receive her weight on her seat.)

Note to Teachers—The possibilities open to the children when using this theme on apparatus are greater than in their work on the floor. The body can be suspended or supported and therefore movements can be made below as well as above the point of support.

B. Weight supported on the arms

TASK 1—Place your hands on the floor and with your weight supported on your arms try to lift different parts of your body high.

TASK 2—Taking your weight on your arms travel lifting different parts of your body high.

(e.g. Seat, one foot after the other, or both feet together.)

Note to Teachers—Refer back to Theme I and emphasise the careful and sensitive reception of the weight onto the feet. Again follow by a neat recovery to standing or with a roll after landing on to the feet.

C. Leg Work

As the body, with the head up, is propelled into the air from a leap or jump, the children can try to lift different parts high.

TASK 1—Run, jump or leap, lifting the head, chest or hands high.

TASK 2—Run and leap, lifting one part of your leg higher than the rest of the same leg.

TASK 3—Run and leap, showing clearly one part of the leg high. Continue trying to lift the same part of the other leg even higher.

Note to Teachers—Discretion is necessary when using these ideas for jumps from apparatus. It is essential that the children should land on two feet if their safety is to be ensured. Only children who are well co-ordinated and can land correctly from easier types of jumps should attempt them.

Sequences can be made combining a task from A, B and C, e.g. from a starting position curled up on the floor the child may lift her seat high, come down receiving her weight on her seat, roll over, jump up, place her hands on the floor and lift her feet high one after the other, come down landing one foot after the other, roll over backwards, jump up and continue into a run and leap lifting her heels high behind her. On landing, she should show a good finish; she is then ready to repeat these movements remembering exactly what she did. (See page 9.)

THEME III
CURLING AND STRETCHING

In curling up all parts of the body close in to the centre and in stretching extend fully away from the centre. In addition the body can be stretched out from the point of support but this may not necessarily mean that the whole body is extended. For example, if a child is supported on her shoulders, her hips and legs will be extended but not her shoulders and head. She is answering the task in that she is stretching her body as far as possible from that point of support.

(*c*) a stretch followed by a twist into a curled position (Theme III).

B. Weight supported on the arms

TASK 1—From a balance on your hands with your seat or feet high, bring your feet down to the floor by using a twist of your body.

TASK 2—Use a twist to place the hands on the floor to left or right of the body and take the weight on the arms.

TASK 3—Travel about the room, using both straight movements and twists.

C. Leg work

TASK 1—Run and leap using a twist of the shoulders or hips in order to make the body land sideways or backwards.

TASK 2—Run, leap and twist in the air:

(*a*) Lift the heels back, looking over one shoulder at them.

(*b*) Use a swing of the leg to lift and twist the body in the air so that a landing is made on the opposite foot.

(*c*) Use a swing of the leg to lift the body, followed by a twist of the shoulders while the body is in the air, landing on the same foot.

Sequences of movement combining A, B and/or C can be used. Movements in which no twist is made can be alternated with those using one. This contrast gives emphasis to the theme and adds interest and variety.

THEME V

SHAPE

The clarity given to a movement by the shape which the body makes is important. Holding or passing through definite shapes gives formality of design. These shapes are the long narrow extended, the wide sideways extended and the compact rounded shapes. Twisting movements can be used in linking the change from shape to shape and if these are held the body will show twisted shapes.

A. The whole body

TASK 1—Using different points of support hold any one of these shapes.

TASK 2—Show as many shapes as you can with the same part of your body supporting you.

TASK 3—Travel about the floor and make your body move continuously through these shapes.

B. Weight supported on the arms

TASK 1—Balance on your hands and try to show these shapes.

Task 2—While taking the weight on your hands try to show two or three of these shapes.

TASK 3—Travel holding a shape whilst on your hands or pass through a shape whilst moving from hands to feet.

C. Leg work

TASK 1—Run, leap and show a definite shape with your body in flight.

N.B.—Safety precaution: the head must be lifted in all jumps.

Sequences can be worked out using combinations of tasks from sections A, B and/or C.

THEME VI
SYMMETRY AND ASYMMETRY

If the body is divided by an imaginary vertical line there will be corresponding parts on either side, thus in symmetrical movement the corresponding parts of the body are used at the same time and in the same way, e.g. both hands are placed on the ground together, both feet are used in the take off, the weight is equally balanced on both shoulders, in flight, both legs or arms are held or lifted in a similar design. In asymmetrical movement the corresponding part of the body is not used in a similar way at the same moment.

The terms symmetrical and asymmetrical whilst clearly expressing the idea of the theme will not be familiar to children. Their persistent use throughout a lesson can have an irritating effect as the words have an artificial sound and suitable alternative ones should be selected to convey their meaning. For this reason, in the first few tasks the idea is expressed in a variety of ways. As, however, symmetrical and asymmetrical indicate clearly to the teacher what is wanted, the remainder of the tasks are given in this form. It is hoped that the teacher will, herself, use a wide vocabulary to explain the tasks.

A. The whole body

TASK 1—Use balance positions, selecting those in which you are equally supported on corresponding parts of the body. In holding the balance make sure that each arm and each leg matches the other. (Symmetrical.)

TASK 2—Use balance positions selecting those in which you use one side of your body or the other to support you, you should never be on two similar parts at the same moment nor should your arms and/or your legs match. (Asymmetrical.)

TASK 3—Travel receiving and supporting your weight symmetrically.

TASK 4—Travel receiving and supporting your weight asymmetrically.

TASK 5—Make up a sequence travelling and using symmetrical movements.

TASK 6—Make up a sequence travelling and using asymmetrical movements.

TASK 7—Make up a sequence which combines both symmetrical and asymmetrical movement in travelling, balancing or receiving the weight.

B. Weight supported on the arms

TASK 1—Travel on the hands and feet with a symmetrical use of the hands.

TASK 2—Travel on the hands and feet with an asymmetrical use of the hands.

TASK 3—Combine the two above tasks to make a sequence.

TASK 4—Practise taking your weight on your hands with an asymmetrical take off from your feet.

TASK 5—As above with a symmetrical take off.

TASK 6—As 4 and 5 above practise symmetrical and asymmetrical landings.

Symmetrical and asymmetrical positions of the body can be used while balanced on the hands.

C. Leg work

TASK 1—Run and leap using a symmetrical take off and landing.

TASK 2—Run and leap using an asymmetrical take off and a symmetrical landing.

TASK 3—Run and leap using an asymmetrical take off and landing.

TASK 4—Run and leap using a symmetrical take off and an asymmetrical landing.

TASK 5—Run and leap using different symmetrical positions in flight.

TASK 6—Run and leap using different asymmetrical positions in flight.

Task 7—Make up a sequence which uses a symmetrical take off and landing and an asymmetrical position in flight.

Sequences combining any of these ideas can be made.

GROUP II—FOR SECONDARY GIRLS

ADVANCED THEMES AND IDEAS FOR THE TEACHER TO DEVELOP INTO THEMES

THEME VII

EMPHASIS PLACED ON SELECTED PARTS OF THE BODY

Interest can be gained by stressing the use of a particular part of the body. The class can be asked to make up a sequence using several points of support and to note and stress what a particular part is doing throughout. (e.g. Legs, hips, knees, feet.)

Choice of the part of the body to be stressed can, in the main, be determined by observation of the class. Postural defects or an inability to do certain movements, which may be due to a lack of sensitivity or to muscular weakness in that part of the body, should be noted. Stress placed on these parts could help to eliminate these weaknesses.

Some examples of this would be:

(i) Poor foot work or lack of spring can be due to weak feet, or to a lack of appreciation of how the feet can be moved and are best used.

(ii) Consciousness of the importance of the lifting of the breast bone can improve posture and enable girls to attain a feeling of lightness.

(iii) Concentration on the abdominal region can help to overcome muscular weakness as well as encourage the girls to appreciate the importance of fixing the spine when the body is thrust into the air in a jump. For instance, in a strong leap, height and grace are lost if the waist is allowed to sag.

THEME VIII

RHYTHM AND PHRASING

Great satisfaction may be experienced from working to a rhythm, and any of the following tasks can be developed into work in pairs or in groups:

(a) starting and finishing together;

(b) working alternately picking up the rhythm;

(c) working in cannon—one start and continue, the next pick up the phrase and so on until all are working and then stop one after the other at the end of the phrase.

Many of the ideas in this theme can be used in conjunction with the other themes.

A. The whole body

Clap a rhythmical phrase set by the teacher or by one of the class.

TASK 1—Make up a sequence transferring your weight from one part of your body to another which will fit this rhythm. Now move to a different rhythm set by another person.

TASK 2—Make up a 'whole body' sequence on any one of the movement ideas of the other themes which will fit the set rhythm.

TASK 3—Work with a partner on any of the previous tasks.

37

(*a*) Together

or (*b*) Alternately

or (*c*) Combination of *a* and *b*.

TASK 4—As task 3 but one partner set the rhythm.

B. Weight supported on the arms

TASK 1—Move and take your weight on your arms and recover to a standing position by a jump up or a roll and repeat your sequence continuously and rhythmically (to the rhythm set by the teacher).

N.B.—Many of the tasks in this section of the other themes can be used in a similar way.

C. Leg work

TASK 1—(Teacher or girl set a rhythm.)

Make up a series of runs and jumps to fit this rhythm and remember the various ways you can use your feet.

N.B.—If the rhythms are suitably chosen a large variety of movements should result.

TASK 2—As Task 1, but turn in the air as you jump.

Sequences—

(1) Sequences combining A and/or B and/or C can be evolved to suit the rhythms set.

(2) Let the girls make up any sequence they like, but with a well-marked rhythm. Choose a girl to show her sequence and then to clap her rhythm. Let all the class make up a sequence to that rhythm.

(3) In twos. Choose a rhythm. Evolve movements under A, B or C, or combining A and/or B and/or C, and arrange to work rhythmically with your partner doing the same or different movements or sequences. Remember you can work:

(*a*) at the same time as your partner;

(*b*) alternately;

(*c*) in cannon;

(*d*) combining (*a*), (*b*) or (*c*).

And also that:

(*a*) you can meet and part from your partner;

(*b*) you can go round your partner;

(c) you can travel on interesting paths, making floor patterns in combination with your partner. The changes of direction can be worked into the phrases of your movement.

Groups instead of pairs can carry out many of these suggestions. Many ideas, particularly under (c), can be worked out with a partner, using a hoop placed on the ground or a beating board or a form.

THEME IX
CIRCLINGS, SWINGINGS AND THE USE OF MOMENTUM

With the use of momentum girls can often find the means of accomplishing feats quite impossible for them to perform by muscular strength alone. This momentum can be imparted by swinging the limbs or the whole body, by making use of swings on ropes and by use of a run.

In the preliminary stages the children learned that by rolling or 'giving' in landing they could lose the momentum they had gained through running and jumping. Theme I, on 'Management of Weight,' is mainly devoted to this study. At an early stage, also, they learn not to misuse momentum. A child will use momentum, giving a run or a swing of the arms and body, to help her get up to a hand-stand position or to get over in a roll. The danger of this method is that the momentum can only be dissipated and not controlled, and once the child gets up to the desired position movement will continue, and she will be in danger of pitching over on her back.

At this more advanced stage the girls can learn how to make use of momentum. Particularly good use can be made of swinging ropes to reach heights difficult to reach by climbing or pulling up.

A. The whole body

TASK 1—Choose two suitable parts of your body and rock from one to the other. Rock backwards and forwards with increasing impetus until you let this carry you right through one of the rocking points, and as you go over allow yourself to continue to roll until the impetus is lost, or twist to continue rocking on the same or different parts.

TASK 2—Lying stretched out rock from side to side until you gain enough impetus to roll over several times.

TASK 3—Sitting with your feet off the ground, make use of a twist of your body and swing of your arms to make you spin round on your seat like a top. Can you spin round on any other parts of your body?

(This task is helpful in illustrating the movement which a swing can bring about, but should be used for this purpose only.)

B. Weight supported on the arms

TASK 1—Crouch down with the weight on your hands and feet. Lift one leg backwards with a straight knee, swing this leg down and up several times, then use it, with a strong swing, to take you up into a hand-stand position.

See if you can use the swing of your leg to initiate any other movement in which you take the weight on your arms.

C. Leg work

TASK 1—Starting with your feet together, see how far and high you can jump and land on two feet. Now start swinging your arms backwards and forwards and give little springing movements in your knees; increase the size of these movements and then give an extra large swing of the arms and spring at the same time. See if you are jumping further and higher than before.

TASK 2—Stand with feet apart (sideways) and sway from foot to foot—now, as you sway, twist your body from side to side and let both arms swing across in front of you from side to side as your body twists. Gradually make this swinging and twisting movement bigger until it spins you round—find all the interesting things you can do once you have started to spin; now see if your swing can take you into a jump.

TASK 3—Standing—Swing your leg with easy heavy movements in various directions. Now see if you can use any of these swings to initiate a movement or jump. You may give a preliminary run and/or jump if you wish. Your swing may well lead you into some sort of twisting or turning movement.

N.B.—Application to Apparatus

Arrange the apparatus carefully and make especial use of ropes. Let the girls find all sorts of ways in which they can hang from the apparatus and swing. Let them gradually increase the range of their swings so that they can appreciate how much further they can reach if they want to bridge a gap, than they could otherwise do.

It is possible for the girls to suspend or support themselves by or on various parts and swing the free part(s) of the body. Then try gradually increasing the range of the swing until a point is reached whence they can stretch out and reach another part or different piece of the apparatus, possibly bridging a gap to do so. Alternatively, a thrust away from the apparatus at the right moment will enable the body to be propelled into the air with considerable force and, therefore, travel with sufficient speed to enable the landings to be made at some distance from the apparatus.

1. It is possible to swing the body or limbs:
   (i) hanging from the hands;
   (ii) supported on the arms between two parallel beams;
   (iii) hanging from first one hand and then the other;
   (iv) suspended by the back of the knees.

2. Strong swinging movements of one or two legs can be used to assist many movements or to or over apparatus or from one part of the apparatus to another.

3. Rocking between two points of support is another possibility. In the group work the arrangement of the apparatus will need to provide suitable opportunities for bridging gaps by the use of swings.

The experience gained in this theme can be usefully employed when working on any of the other themes.

THEME X

SUCCESSIVE AND SIMULTANEOUS MOVEMENT

This can be used with the older and more able girls. This idea should stimulate interesting movements in which the girls

41

draw on former experience from other themes and show these two contrasting ways of moving.

A successive movement is a wave-like one in which movement flows through the body, one part moving after the other. A clear example of this would be a stretching out of the body, in which the stretch gradually flows through each successive part until a full stretch is obtained. It can be done from the feet to the hands, or from the centre of the body out to the extremities of the limbs.

A simultaneous movement is one in which all parts of the body move and reach their destination at the same moment.

Taken on its own as a theme this idea might prove limiting. Rather should it be applied to a theme already mastered, particularly in the whole body and arm work and transferred where possible on to the apparatus. The value of this type of movement is that it encourages body and movement awareness. Increased sensitivity and suppleness should result. Much useful work can be done with girls who have a lifelessness and rigidity in the spine. Older girls derive aesthetic pleasure from moving in this way.

THEME XI
PARTS OF THE BODY LEADING THE MOVEMENT

Many purposeful and objective movements and sequences can be made with the idea of different parts of the body leading the movement as the main theme of a lesson. Used with girls who have reached a stage in the work when the movement training part of the lesson is spent mainly on sequence and partner work, it is a valuable addition to their experience. For example, parts of the body can lead the way in various directions before taking the body weight, or they can be used to guide a twisting movement or to lead as the shape of the body alters in movement. Care should be taken to encourage objective work rather than expressive gestures and dance-like actions.

THEME XII
LOSING AND RECOVERING BALANCE

This theme should only be taken with a class which has bodily skill and control. Lessons at first should be devoted to finding the points of support for the body over which it is difficult to maintain the centre of gravity. The maintenance of a balance position becomes increasingly difficult:

(a) when the area of the part supporting the body is reduced.

(b) as the points of support, if small, approach a straight line.

From positions of this kind balance can be lost by extending a limb farther out into space and so drawing the body off balance, or by allowing the whole body to lean until it falls off balance. The skill demanded then is the ability to ' catch ' or receive the weight with safety often making use of momentum and rolling.

Certain points must be stressed with the children:

(i) They must think ahead and know which part of their body is going to take their weight first and where the movement will take them.

(ii) The longer the moment of overbalance is delayed, the more important it is to know which part of the body will receive the weight and to prepare accordingly.

(iii) There must be an initial ' give ' or softness and relaxation as the weight is received.

(iv) They must have the ability to control their bodies and react quickly so that they can adjust and adapt their bodies to the right shape for falling and receiving their weight in the best position for landing.

Care must be taken in applying this idea to the apparatus as the safety of the girls should be our foremost consideration. It can be used with least risk in over-balancing from forms or a low box as the nearness of the floor, provided the surrounding space is left free, will enable them to roll with safety.

Partner and Group Work

Partner and Group work are valuable because:

(1) it adds interest to the work;

(2) each child can learn new movements from her partner or groups;

(3) each child learns to adapt the manner in which she moves to that of her partner or group;

(4) it demands accuracy of observation followed by accuracy of performance;

43

(5) socially the child learns co-operation and must be able both to lead and to follow.

This work is a development that can be based on the themes and, therefore, a sufficient number of themes should be covered before it is introduced.

ASPECTS OF WORK IN PAIRS

1. MATCHING

Partners move simultaneously or one after the other, having worked out the movements to be made. They can match each other as a pair by working:

(a) side by side;
(b) one behind the other;
(c) facing each other;
(d) independently using different paths and approaching at different angles;
(e) towards and away from each other.

2. CONTRASTING

Using suitable movements, partners work in contrast to each other.

3. PARTNERS AS OBSTACLES

Partners may use each other as obstacles and move over, under or round each other in various ways. Their movement should be complementary, though they need not match.

4. MOVEMENTS WITH PARTNERS IN CONTACT

(a) After finding ways of supporting each other they should build up sequences in which they travel. They should use these methods of support purposefully with suitable linking movements.

(b) Supporting and helping a partner to take her weight on different parts of her own body. This may be active or passive help, i.e. the partner may make movements which definitely assist in the taking of weight or she may remain stationary.

(c) One partner lifts, holds and lowers, with absolute control, the entire weight of the other in various ways. (Should only be used with advanced performers.)

44

(*d*) Partners counterbalance the weight of each other, i.e. a position is held and a movement is carried out with the balance of each entirely dependent on the grip or support of the other.

(*e*) Assisting a partner's flight in different ways.

ASPECTS OF WORK IN THREES

Variations can be achieved by the way in which the group is arranged.

1. Matching, simultaneous movement of all three.
2. The three arranged as two and one, all using complementary movements.
3. Working individually and using movements which assist each other or complement the floor pattern or rhythm of the others.
4. Working on matching movements but made in cannon.
5. Assisting, by one helping two or two helping one; this would include different kinds of contacts, grips and lifts, as well as throwing and catching each other. (Should only be attempted with skilled and advanced performers.)

CHAPTER IV

THE FOUR MOVEMENT FACTORS

Children should experience in a simple way the effects which the use of the factors of Time, Space, Weight or Flow (Continuity) have on an action before applying them to tasks and sequences.

I—TIME

Any movement uses a quantity of time—it may be quick using little time, or slow using much time. The speed of a movement or movement sequence need not be uniform throughout. Variation of speed may be developed into a rhythmic pattern. Movements may also be sudden or sustained. In gymnastics either may be used for perfecting a technique, often to assist in the recovery of balance, or the reception of weight, or to add to the interest or difficulty of a movement.

Before asking for variations of time in a sequence it is often useful for the children to perform their own sequences several times as quickly as they can (with safety) and then as slowly as possible. From these experiences a child will learn which parts are best done quickly or slowly and which can be done equally well at any speed. She should then be asked to repeat her sequence with changes of speed in appropriate places.

Time as a Theme

To give the children useful experience a whole lesson can be taken with Time as a theme. This can be attempted in the first place when the children have some knowledge of moving in a variety of ways. The teacher should use the same plan of lesson selecting simple tasks from one or more of the themes and ask the children to introduce a certain aspect of the time factor.

The Use of Time with Movement Sequences and Tasks

Sequences or tasks may be performed:
  (i) at a speed which may be uniformly quick or slow, or may alternate between quick and slow;
 (ii) with variations of speed, which can be:
      (a) attained gradually and lost gradually,
      (b) attained gradually and lost suddenly,
      (c) attained suddenly and lost gradually;
(iii) with several changes of speed using combinations of any of the above within the sequence.

II—SPACE

The body is surrounded by space into which, from a stationary base, it can extend in all directions and at all levels. This space is known as the 'sphere of movement'. As soon as the body begins to travel it moves into the general space of the room.

Direction

The directions in which the body can move when the trunk is vertical are backwards, forwards, sideways, upwards and downwards; when the trunk is horizontal, head first, feet first and sideways.

The Path

In gymnastics the path is the track which the body makes when travelling about the floor, on the apparatus, or through the air.

Direction as a Theme

Using the 'Plan of lesson' suitable tasks from the themes can be set with direction as an added condition.

Use of Direction with Movement Sequences and Tasks

Sequences and tasks may be performed:
  (i) in one direction only;
 (ii) with variations of direction;
      e.g. (a) moving forwards, change to moving backwards;
           (b) moving sideways, change to moving forwards;
           (c) moving backwards, change to moving sideways.
Many other combinations of directions can be made.

47

Level

Variations in level can give added interest to a movement; in drawing attention to the level of a movement we use the terms high, medium amd low level.

Children often tend to work on one level only and in this case their attention should be drawn to the others which they can use. A theme on level would be helpful at this stage.

Level as a Theme

Again the ' Plan of lesson ' will be used and simple purposeful tasks should be set. It is essential that the children have a vocabulary of movement before attempting this theme.

Use of Level with Movement Sequences and Tasks

Sequences and tasks may be performed:
  (i) on any one level;
 (ii) with variation between two or three levels;
        e.g. (a) starting low, finishing high;
             (b) starting high, finishing low;
             (c) using medium, high and low levels.

When working on the apparatus the two ways of interpreting level should be considered and the children should know and understand which they are using, the task should make this clear. They should consider:

  (a) the height at which they work on the apparatus;
  (b) the height at which the body is from its point of support.

III—WEIGHT—(FORCE—STRENGTH)

A degree of strength is needed to produce any movement. In gymnastics, the understanding of this weight factor must be directed towards the functional purpose of the movement, as the amount of strength needed varies according to the height of the apparatus and to the manner in which the body is propelled, pulled up, on or over it. The exertion of full muscular power for any movement involving the whole body should be preceded by a strong tension in the abdominal muscles. The effectiveness of a ' take-off ' from a spring board is reduced if the body is not kept firm by this tension of the abdominal muscles, so that the thrust of the legs can be transmitted through the body.

Children should be trained to apply muscle power economically by using the appropriate degree of strength for a particular movement and by avoiding unnecessary tension in other parts of the body. In the upright position on the floor, apparatus or in flight a feeling of lightness may be induced by lifting the chest upwards.

The term weight here covers not only the use made of the weight of the body but also the muscular action which together enable the child to move with varying degrees of strength or lightness. As a factor of movement weight is related to the effort and control of the body through degrees of muscular tension.

There are three aspects of weight:

(i) Strength,   i.e. strong muscular tension
(ii) Lightness, i.e. light muscular tension
(iii) Heaviness, i.e. release of muscular tension or relaxation.

The degree of relaxation will depend on the extent to which muscular tension is released.

A well performed skilful movement is one in which the correct degree of strength or lightness is used, thus producing both efficiency and economy of effort. When effort control is poor there is an ineffective and uneconomical use of muscular tension, e.g. holding on to a strong effort too long results in fatigue and strain. Conversely ' letting go ' too soon results in flopping, or crashing down with lack of control, the body not having been given sufficient time to prepare to receive the weight.

Preparation—Action—Recovery

Every action should have three phases:

(i) a preparation;
(ii) a stressed action;
(iii) a recovery.

The preparation is necessary for the right positioning of the limbs and body for the most effective use of the weight of the body in carrying out the action. The recovery is necessary because without it a movement cannot continue over a long period without strain. Practice and observation will show that it is extremely difficult to hold on with the same degree of muscular

49

tension for any length of time without some deterioration in that muscular effort. If, however, recovery movements are inserted it is possible to continue without strain and without deterioration both of effort and intention. Children should be made aware, in the more advanced stages of their training, of these three phases in an action and should be encouraged to show clearly the contrast between the strongly accented actions and the lighter or relaxed movements which intervene.

Accents

In gymnastics the climax of the lesson is devoted to finding solutions to problems related to a theme whilst using settings of apparatus. For this it is necessary at times to lift the body in various ways on to or over the apparatus, and this cannot be done without changes of strength. For this reason practice in stressing or accenting certain parts of the movement may help in achieving this.

Accents may be of the strong, slow pushing, pressing, pulling or twisting type showing sustained strength, or they may be of the urgent, sudden, thrusting, punching or slashing type showing drive and force.

If children have the opportunity of experiencing and understanding the importance of the changes in muscular effort their muscular skill and control should grow. Some may begin to show ' quality ' of movement, i.e. a feeling of energy, drive and decisiveness when using strength, controlled quietness or calm lightness when using slow, light muscular tension, or a briskness and nimbleness in quick, light movements.

Movement Training Work on the Floor

In this work children can:

(i) decide where, in their completed sequences, accents need to be placed;

(ii) make up sequences which show a series of quick, strong or slow strong accents;

(iii) make up sequences which include contrasts of quick, strong and slow strong accents.

Some interesting work can develop if they make up sequences which:

(i) start with light, slow movements and build up with gradually increasing speed and power into final strong accent;

(ii) start with a strong, slow or explosive movement and die away in a light, quiet movement;

(iii) build up in strength, explode, and die away;

(iv) have a simple series of phrases of movement with a repetitive accent throughout the sequence. (Rhythmic pattern.)

IV—FLOW

This movement factor is concerned with control, and the two extremes are bound flow and free flow.

Bound Flow

A bound flow movement is one in which the effort control is such that the movement can be stopped at any point. The ability to arrest or steady a movement is an essential part of skilful body management. Too much concentration on bound flow may lead to lack of fluency and then movements become a series of positions.

An understanding of bound flow may be gained by performing sequences in which the action can be checked or controlled at selected points and a balanced position and clearly defined body shape is shown.

Free Flow

The contrasting aspect of bound flow is free flow. In this control is lacking and the flow of movement can only be stopped with difficulty. In gymnastics safety is essential and emphasis is placed on continuity of movement rather than on free flow. Continuity of movement calls for a skilful joining together of a series of different actions into an easily flowing and logical sequence of movements, in such a way that no involuntary pauses or breaks appear throughout the whole movement pattern. To do this successfully the use of unstable points of support make the fluent transition from one action into another easier; however, a change of direction can sometimes help to keep the movement continuous should a stable point of support be used. For example, it quite often happens with beginners that a child will use a

51

movement which will take her into a face downward position lying on the floor and then try to go in a forward or backward direction which is not possible without a break in the continuity. If, however, she were to change direction and roll sideways on to her back she can then use a forward or backward movement without any check or pause.

The moment children begin to work on sequences, combining jumps with weight bearing on the arms as well as transferring their weight on to other parts of the body, the need for fluency arises. It is here that the teacher can give individual help and can also make use of class observation. She could either suggest more logical transitions from one action to the other; or she could ask the class to work out a solution to the difficulty they have observed.

The understanding and use of these two aspects of movement is most valuable. They can be used as a theme, giving the children an opportunity to feel the difference in quality. The class should be encouraged to use sequences in which the transition from one point of support to another is fluent, smooth and rhythmical and then to use those in which the flow is purposely checked or controlled at selected points, balancing the body and showing a clearly defined shape.

Combination of various aspects of the Movement Factors

Two aspects of one of the factors of Time, Space, Weight and Flow or one aspect of any two factors can be used in tasks. The ability to do this marks an advanced stage in the training.

A few examples are:

Space (combination of two aspects of one factor).

Move at a low level in one direction and at a high level in another direction.

Time with Space (combination of an aspect of time with an aspect of space).

(i) Move quickly in one direction and slowly in another.

(ii) Move slowly at a low and quickly at a high level (or the reverse).

(iii) Move quickly upwards and slowly downwards (or the reverse).

CHAPTER V

OBSERVATION

Keen observation is of the greatest importance in movement education both from the point of view of the teacher and of the children. Analysing movement in terms of Time, Weight, Space and Flow and basing her observation on these, the teacher can detect faults and give the appropriate guidance and correction to both the individual child and the group. A child trained in observation should be able to improve her own skill in movement and later may be able to help others.

1. The teacher should move about the room in order to observe and give individual help; she must at the same time be aware of what is happening in all parts of the room. At some stage she must position herself in order to observe the movement of the whole class.

2. She should observe:
   (i) whether the children are fulfilling the task purposefully and she should be prepared to help individually those whose work is lacking in this respect;
   (ii) if the children's work has made real demands upon them;
   (iii) if the work of any child could be used to demonstrate a teaching point she wishes to make.

3. Observation should enable her to assess the needs of the class in order to develop the work within the present lesson and for future lessons. These needs should be recorded in the lesson notes.

4. The teacher should use her discretion in the amount of time spent by the children on observation in any lesson, bearing in mind that it should be a period of physical activity and that the pace of a lesson is of great importance. Interest and enjoyment will be lost if too much time is given to demonstration.

Children need to be trained in observation and at first will be slow to see what is required. In the early stages, therefore, they may be asked to observe only one point in a movement. There is a danger that the most spectacular performers will be asked to demonstrate too often. Opportunity should be found for children of differing physical types to show their solution to the task which though simple may illustrate effectively a particular point.

SAFETY PRECAUTIONS

The safety of the children must be the first consideration at all times.

Accommodation

   (i)   Choice of activity must be governed by the size of the hall.
 (ii)   The floor should be kept as clean and splinter-proof as possible and should not be slippery.
(iii)   All furniture which cannot be removed from the hall must be placed safely or stacked in suitable positions, freeing the largest space possible for the children.

       The teacher should note the likely ' danger spots ' (sharp corners, hot-plates, etc.) and guard against them*.

Clothing

The use of suitable gymnastic clothing is essential and bare foot work is safe and desirable where the floor is in good condition and splinter-proof. Socks only or hard-soled shoes must not be worn.

The Apparatus

   (i)   Each piece of apparatus must be in sound condition, e.g. no splinters, torn surfaces or stitching, highly polished leather, unsteady supports, etc.
 (ii)   The children should receive careful instruction in the handling of apparatus in order to prevent damage to themselves, the apparatus or the floor. They should be trained to assemble it correctly and should be prepared

---

*The Ministry of Education Pamphlet No. 13, ' Safety Precautions in Schools,' contains a section on precautions for Physical Education. The book is published by Her Majesty's Stationery Office at 17½p.

to make any necessary adjustments at any time during the lesson.

(iii) The apparatus should be arranged in the room to allow adequate space for the approach to, and completion of, any task and to avoid collision with adjacent sections.

(iv) Children should be trained to avoid obstructing or interfering with other members of the class when moving back to their place or waiting for a turn.

(v) Mats should be provided when the height from which, or the speed with which, the child lands, calls for their use.

Finally, tasks set on the apparatus must not produce results demanding a greater degree of skill in the management of their weight than the children possess (see Theme I).

THE USE AND ORGANISATION OF THE APPARATUS

Use during the Introduction and Movement Training section of the Lesson

Here the apparatus is used to help the movement and/or to give some progression; for example, forms may be used to jump on and off in order to increase the height of the jump.

In ideal circumstances no child should be waiting for a turn; the degree to which this can be attained depends on an adequate supply of apparatus and the space available. In small halls skilful arrangement of the apparatus is necessary to ensure safety of movement. Lack of space may be overcome if some children hold apparatus and/or observe others at work. When apparatus is used in this section of the lesson the same task will be set for the whole class.

Small apparatus (hoops, ropes and canes) should only be used as obstacles to get over, under, round or through. The skills, such as throwing and catching a ball, should be taken in a games lesson and where possible out of doors.

Use in the Climax of the Lesson

The purpose of the apparatus here is to provide a challenging climax to the lesson. Again it is most important to see that as many children as possible are working within the bounds of safety. Queues should be avoided and ideally each group should consist of only three or four children. This can often be achieved by having two groups working simultaneously at one piece of apparatus such as a mat and/or form. This organisation, to provide maximum activity, needs careful thought and planning before the lesson. A diagram of how the apparatus is to be set out is most important and every teacher should include this in the preparation of the lesson.

The use and arrangement of the apparatus will be governed by the theme of the lesson and the tasks set. Tasks can be set in two different ways:

    (i)   All groups have the same tasks but work at different pieces of apparatus.

    (ii) A different task is given to each group.

In choosing the arrangements of apparatus to suit particular tasks, combinations of various pieces can be made, e.g. form leading up to a box; forms, mats and climbing ropes; canes, hoops and mats. The task set will not necessarily involve the same line of approach to the apparatus by each child.

During a series of lessons devoted to a theme and before a new theme is introduced, children should have had the opportunity to explore, select and perfect an activity at each arrangement of apparatus, thus attaining a good standard of performance. In any one lesson the children will probably only work at one or two sections.

Progression in the Use of Apparatus

1.   When the apparatus has been set out and a task or tasks have been given, the children may choose at which grouping of apparatus they will work. They will be free to move to other groups once they have achieved a standard of performance at their first choice. The give and take in the avoidance of queues makes valuable social demands upon the children.

2.   A task may be set on the lesson theme and each group of children make their own arrangement of the apparatus allocated to them.

3.   The apparatus is set out and the children make up their own tasks on the theme of the lesson.

THE LIFTING OF APPARATUS

Constant lifting and lowering of heavy objects is part of the daily routine, yet it is not always realised that there is a correct and incorrect way of lifting. Much unnecessary injury is caused, particularly to the back, through lack of this knowledge.

The moving of the apparatus offers a valuable opportunity for practical training in lifting. With the older girls it would be useful if before they leave school, some time were devoted during lessons to the application of the principles of safe lifting, pushing and pulling, to the situations they are likely to meet in the home or at work, i.e. moving furniture, lifting heavy buckets, gardening, etc. In brief, firstly, it is important that when lifting heavy objects the spine should be fixed in its normal position and that the power for the lift should come primarily from the legs. This means that the knees must be well bent if picking up an object from the floor. Secondly, that in pushing or pulling heavy objects the weight of the whole body should be behind the action.

A booklet, 'Housework with Ease',* gives in a simple form the knowledge required.

PROGRESSION

The way in which the work is developed may well vary from teacher to teacher. What is important is that each one should have a clear picture of how she will build up the girls' vocabulary of movement and help them to transfer and apply their ideas to the apparatus, making sure that they use it suitably and fully. With growing experience, as with speech, they will use their language more effectively and with greater understanding, thus adding sensitivity and skilful efficiency to their actions.

Elementary Stage

During this stage the girls are building up a vocabulary of movement. They experience many different aspects in their simplest form, thus learning the language of movement.

---

*' Housework with Ease ', by T. MaClurg Anderson. Published by the Scottish Council of Physical Recreation and in association with the Central Council of Physical Recreation.

They must, first and foremost, acquire skill in the manage ment of their weight on the apparatus. Theme I gives much material on this subject and work on it should be developed until the girls have sufficient skill and confidence to leap boldly on, off and over apparatus. They should show attack in their approach to the apparatus by the confidence and purposefulness of their run and jump, and enjoy the exhilaration that flight can give once there is certainty of the ability to land safely from all situations. They should be able to land safely and with resilience if the landing is to be the preparation for another movement.

Almost from the start when working on Theme I, the teacher will observe where and when she can suggest the use of the movement factors. If the girls always move forwards, can they change direction? If they move with an even rhythm, can they bring in a change of time or strength? If they are constantly on the floor, can they change level?

The girls will become competent in the management of their weight in the floor work of the movement training section of their lessons before they reach a corresponding degree of skill on the apparatus.

Once the teacher is satisfied with the skill of their floor work, she can begin to develop further the girls' vocabulary of move-ment by working on the simpler tasks from one of the themes in Group I, but she should develop the work on the apparatus more slowly. She may first confine the girls to the use of certain sections of the apparatus, or to defined paths of movement and may, perhaps, ask for variations in direction, level or time.

When the girls have a good grasp of the movement idea of the theme of their floor work, they may be encouraged to incor-porate it, if they see an opportunity, into their work on the apparatus.

The movement training may subsequently be based on the simple tasks from other themes in Group I, and be used, as before, with the apparatus, but the work should be growing richer, showing evidence of the experience gained from previous themes as well as from the particular lesson.

The girls should be reaching a stage when tasks can be set on the apparatus which make more specific demands and should be encouraged to be more disciplined in the use of their movement ideas. They should travel on selected paths while using the ideas from the theme and in doing this be able to produce a continuous, logical and efficient sequence of movements. Should the demands cause any loss of attack or a marked reduction of flight or movement over the apparatus, then the girls are not yet ready for this progression, and more work should be done on Theme I.

The Advanced Stage

It is assumed at this stage that the girls now have a good vocabulary of movement and are able to make up skilful and logical sequences both on the floor and the apparatus. In their sequence work they should be encouraged to use freely any aspects of the movement factors, and once able to do so they should be expected to use them purposefully not only to enhance the interest of the movement but to give greater efficiency to their actions.

In both the floor and apparatus work the inclusion of partner and group work will grow. In the movement training section of the lesson increasing use will be made of forms and mats and movement with partners in contact may be developed to an advanced stage.

The use of themes from Group II should give opportunities for the production of work of a really high standard apart from work on these themes and on others of comparable difficulty developed by the teacher. To an increasing extent the girls may be allowed to decide upon their own tasks and, often working in pairs or groups, may build up their work over a series of lessons, the final result being work of good calibre involving a high degree of co-operation and group awareness.

In the foregoing paragraphs an attempt has been made to show how the content of this handbook might be used to form a progressive scheme of work throughout the years, and to give a composite picture which may enable the teacher to assess the progress each lesson has brought. It is hoped that it may help the teachers to produce skilful results, satisfying not only to the girls but also to herself as the culmination of her own thoughtful and intelligent teaching.

If the girls have reaped the benefit of this work they should leave school not only with the knowledge of having attained good standards but also with pleasurable recollections of their time in the gymnasium. They should be aware of the self-confidence which this work can engender and of the satisfaction that can be won in overcoming difficulties. They should take with them an understanding of movement which will help them to undertake as efficiently and effortlessly as possible, the many physical tasks which their life in the home or at work will present.

Supplied to Inner London Education Authority by Greater London Council Supplies Department
Printing and Graphic Design Division and printed by Sir J. Causton & Sons Limited, London
(63207—A43135) 3/72

HOW TO PRODUCE YOUR OWN VIDEOCONFERENCE

Georgia A. Mathis

Knowledge Industry Publications, Inc.
White Plains, NY and London

Video Bookshelf

How to Produce Your Own Videoconference

Library of Congress Cataloging-in-Publication Data

Mathis, Georgia A.
  How to produce your own videoconference.

  Bibliography: p.
  Includes index.
  1. Teleconferencing.   I. Title.
TK5102.5.M298   1986   384   86-21430
ISBN 0-86729-216-4

Printed in the United States of America

10   9   8   7   6   5   4   3   2   1

Contents

List of Tables and Figures v
Acknowledgments vii

  1. Videoconferencing: An Overview 1
  2. Identifying Applications 17
  3. Justifying the Cost 25
  4. Planning and Preparation 37
  5. The Production Process: Pre-Production Elements . . . 47
  6. The Production Process: From Rehearsal to On-Air . . 65
  7. Networking 79
  8. Meeting Site Considerations 99
  9. Managing the Project 113
10. Remaining in Control on the Day of the Event 121
11. After the Event 135

Appendix A: Broadcast Checklist 141
Appendix B: Cost Justification Worksheet 143
Appendix C: Service Confirmation Form—A/V and
               Downlink 145
Appendix D: Service Confirmation Form—Meeting Sites 147
Appendix E: Sample Site Facilitator's Guide 149
Appendix F: Site Checklist 155
Appendix G: Evaluation Form 157

Bibliography 159
Index 161
About the Author 165

List of Tables and Figures

Figure 1.1   A satellite footprint   4
Figure 1.2   A videoconference network   6
Figure 1.3   Smith Kline & French Laboratories
             executives   13

Figure 2.1   Talent rehearsing in the studio   20

Table 3.1   A 21-Site Videoconference Budget   26
Figure 3.1   A panel of executives responding to
             questions   30
Table 3.2   Comparative Costs of a Videoconference
             and Face-to-Face Meeting   31

Figure 5.1   Using a teleprompter   56
Figure 5.2   A satellite introduction.   58
Figure 5.3   A live studio audience   59
Table 5.1   Budget for a Typical In-Studio Live
             Videoconference   63

Figure 6.1   Panel of experts   68
Figure 6.2   Screening questions in the phone room   69
Figure 6.3   Panel members responding to questions   70
Figure 6.4   Executive having makeup applied   72

Figure 7.1   A transportable Ku-band uplink   83
Figure 7.2   A transportable uplink dish   85
Figure 7.3   Engineer inside a transportable uplink
             truck   86
Figure 7.4   A roof-mounted fixed downlink   87
Table 7.1   A Twenty-Site Network for a Four-Hour
             Event   95

Figure 8.1   Attorneys participating in an educational
             seminar   101
Figure 8.2   Receive site at the U.S. Chamber of
             Commerce   102

Table 9.1   Videoconference Timetable Air Date-
             October 1   117
Table 9.2   Sample Checkpoint Chart   120

Figure 10.1 Phone room set up to receive questions   132
Figure 10.2 Operators taking questions from audience
             members at remote sites   133

Acknowledgments

My thanks go to the dozens of technicians, production people and hotel personnel who worked patiently with me to make my projects successful.

Special thanks are due to those who willingly agreed to lengthy interviews to fill in the gaps in my perspective. Their names are found in the text.

Most important, this book would not have been possible without the assistance and encouragement of my family, Jill Witofsky and John Court—I lovingly thank them.

1

Videoconferencing: An Overview

The objective of this book is to give you a practical guide to producing your own videoconference. While we recognize that every possible contingency may not be covered here, the information contained should provide enough substance to allow you to solve your special problems. The bibliography, found at the back, provides a list of additional resources that will help you fill in the gaps.

This book is written for the individual who has at least some small familiarity with audiovisual production. There is no intention here to teach the art of television production or the technical details of satellite communications. Rather, the idea is to provide a workable approach to the management of a videoconference.

It seems appropriate at this point to define what—for the purpose of this book—is meant by a videoconference. It is defined here as a closed-circuit, point-to-multipoint broadcast-quality television program that is usually produced as a one-time event. This is to distinguish the word from the term "teleconference" which, although it includes videoconferences, encompasses telephone audioconferencing, freeze-frame conferencing and digital "full-motion" conferencing.

Videoconferences are, by their nature, complex projects. Each one involves the interplay of highly sophisticated equipment (television production equipment), uplinks, satellites, downlinks, technicians, production personnel and meeting logistics experts. This array of components would make a project complicated even if all parts of it were to be executed in one easily manageable location. Couple that with the realization that

10, 20, 50 or more remote locations—each with its own set of technical requirements—are also included, and you begin to see why a workable management technique is mandatory.

Many general task categories make up the production of a videoconference project:

- production of a live television show
- arrangement of transmission links that involve uplinks, satellites, microwave interconnections, downlinks and, perhaps, telephone company video landlines
- arrangements for audiovisual reception equipment at receive sites
- arrangements for appropriate meeting space at remote sites
- arrangements for peripheral services at meeting sites, such as food and beverages, sleeping rooms and added audiovisuals
- management of all personnel involved in the tasks listed above

All of these topics will be covered here. Heavy emphasis is placed on planning well and in great detail to help your event progress as smoothly as possible. The idea is to help you avoid problems and retain control of your project.

ABOUT VIDEOCONFERENCING

The advent of satellite communications made videoconferencing possible. Although closed circuit television was being produced and distributed before the age of satellites, the transmission of the television signal was dependent upon telephone company video landlines. This system was, and still is, a point-to-point system. That means that one wire at one location is connected, and carries a signal, to one other location. It takes entire webs of these lines going point to point to point to point, ad infinitum, to connect several simultaneous receive sites.

Until just a few years ago, television networks used this method to interconnect their affiliates. Though expensive, this technique was the only one available, and it was workable. However, with satellites reducing the cost of transmission and the breakup of AT&T resulting in higher prices for using the landline system, the networks made the switch to satellite distribution.

Satellite transmission is less expensive than landline transmission for one basic reason. No physical cables must be laid or maintained. Once a satellite is launched, it is good for 10 or more years of reliable service. Since each satellite has 12, 24 or more transponders (individual transmitters)—with over 20 satellites currently available to domestic U.S. video users—there is plenty of capacity (see Figure 1.1).

This capacity, too, is quite accessible. It is accessible to the originator through long-term leases available to heavy users of satellite time and on an hourly "occasional use" basis to less frequent users, as for most videoconferences. On the receiving side, because of the way a satellite transmits, its signal is accessible from anywhere within the satellite's "footprint" as long as the receive equipment is properly tuned.

This is how video transmission by satellite works: First, a television camera delivers a picture, via a cable or overland microwave signal, to an uplink. This uplink may be colocated with a studio, or it may be miles away.

An uplink is a dish-shaped antenna that transmits microwave signals to a satellite. The uplink is aimed at a particular satellite, and its frequency is tuned to match what the individual satellite transponder expects. This signal is picked up by the transponder, amplified and retransmitted toward earth. In most cases this signal disperses over a wide area of the earth (its footprint) and can be received by any downlink dish (receiver) properly equipped and tuned within that area, regardless of how remote the location. The signal received is strongest at the central points of the footprint and weakens as the edges are reached. Since one footprint cannot cover the entire earth at once (just as the moon cannot shine on all parts of the earth at once) three separate satellites are required to access the entire circumference of the globe simultaneously.

These additional satellites are accessed by "turning around" the original signal. This means that the original transmission is received by a downlink strategically placed with direct access to another uplink, which retransmits the signal to a sec-

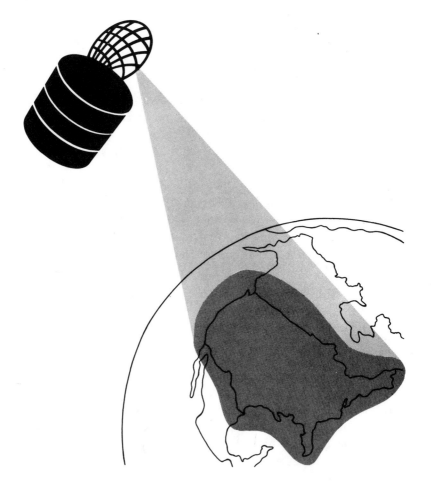

Figure 1.1: A satellite footprint covering the Continental United States (CONUS).

ond satellite, farther along the equator. This is repeated for access to a third satellite, to complete the circle (Figure 1.2).

Satellites are easily reached by uplink signals because they are always in the same location in the sky relative to any given point on earth. This "geostationary" orbit is achieved by placing the satellite in a position about 22,300 miles above the equator. Since it will orbit the globe at the same speed at which the earth rotates, the satellite will always appear to stand still.

DOMESTIC AND INTERNATIONAL TRANSMISSION

Technologically, transmitting a signal internationally is not any more difficult than transmitting domestically. One just needs to use the turnaround procedures outlined above. The relative difficulty comes in the form of regulated access to international transmission. The word *difficulty* may be too strong. The procedure for arranging an international transmission is only a little more complicated than arranging for a domestic broadcast. You can use the capacity quite readily if you follow the rules established by the nations you plan to access.

In the United States (and now, largely, for transmission into Canada) the regulations are quite open. Many companies own satellites (AT&T, RCA, Satellite Business Systems, Western Union, etc.), all competing with each other in price and service for your business. Although you must order satellite time from a common carrier registered with the FCC, these carriers are readily available (Wold, Bonneville, VideoStar, etc.), and they make the regulatory process invisible to the end user. You need only phone one of these companies, order your satellite time, pay your rent, and you're ready to transmit. (See *Teleconferencing Resources Directory* in the Bibliography.) All over the United States, downlinks abound in great numbers—fixed in concrete, mounted on roofs, transported on trailers. These downlinks are found at office buildings, hotels, theaters, convention centers, homes, college campuses, hospitals, car dealerships, etc. All are legal, and many are for rent by the day or hour.

The situation is quite different in most other countries. To access the remainder of the world from the United States, you must—though at this writing some changes are in the works—

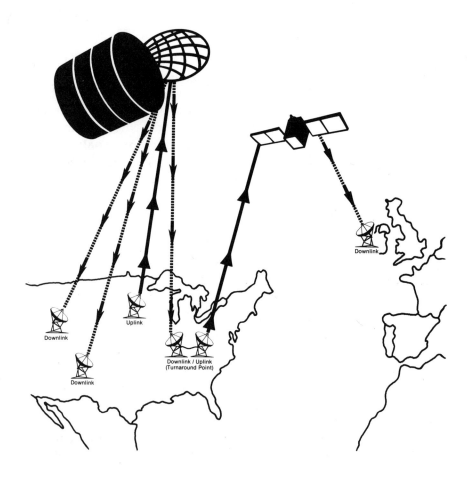

Figure 1.2: A videoconference network with a turnaround to access Europe.

use satellites owned by the International Telecommunications Satellite Organization (INTELSAT). INTELSAT is a consortium of over 100 countries that participate in the operation and regulation of international satellite access. Communications Satellite Corporation (COMSAT) is the U.S. signatory to INTELSAT. Both COMSAT and INTELSAT have offices in the Washington, DC, area. You will find that personnel at both these organizations are quite willing to help you with questions regarding access to overseas locations by satellite.

From the standpoint of U.S. users, however, the help that COMSAT or INTELSAT can give you really ends somewhere over the ocean, where your signal has reached an INTELSAT satellite. From that point the signal must be received by a participating country, and any arrangements you make for reception or rebroadcast to sites within that country are entirely under its regulatory controls. Although there is some sign of loosening controls in many Western European nations, all transmissions outside the United States still fall under the jurisdiction of the state-controlled Post Telephone and Telegraph (PTT) systems.

Each PTT has its own rules and tariffs. Each PTT has its own ideas about whether privately owned downlinks can be used within the country's borders to receive a signal (turned around from the INTELSAT reception onto the individual nation's domestic satellite system) or must be transmitted via PTT-owned and -operated landlines or microwave.

Should your videoconference network include overseas locations, plan on subcontracting your foreign locations with videoconference companies resident in Europe, Japan or wherever your transmission is to be received, unless you have considerable understanding of the operations of the PTTs involved. Otherwise, you may find yourself getting mired in overwhelming detail as you analyze differing rate structures and order services from suppliers with widely varying requirements. Some of these subcontractors have offices in the United States. Viscom International, for example, a British company, has offices in New York. You will find others listed in *The Satellite Directory* and *Video Register and Teleconferencing Resources Directory* (see Bibliography).

When dealing with subcontractors—especially if your contacts are overseas—be prepared to describe exactly what you need. Have all of your requirements laid out before you call; it will save you money. A tremendous amount of cash can be expended in telexes and overseas phone calls. The total can grow geometrically if you need to spend time hashing out "maybe's" and "what if's" with your Paris subcontractor. Follow the planning procedures laid out in this book before making contact.

AD HOC VERSUS FIXED NETWORKS

Videoconference networks are generally divided into two categories, ad hoc and fixed. An ad hoc network is one that is put together for one specific event. It, or at least most of it, does not exist before the broadcast and it is dismantled afterwards. Ad hoc videoconferences are usually special events that need to access a given set of sites once or only occasionally. For example, suppose you want to announce a new product to the press in the cities where your company is conducting its test marketing. You would order downlinks and meeting sites in only those cities and just for the announcement date.

On the other hand, suppose you needed to access the same sites day after day, just as the television networks need to access their affiliates; you would probably install a fixed network. Some hotel chains, such as Holiday Inn, Inc., own and operate networks of downlinks that are permanently installed, or fixed, at their properties. This equipment is available for videoconference use. However, in the strict sense of the term, your videoconference may use this network and still be considered ad hoc in the sense that on one occasion you may access one subset of Holiday Inns and on another occasion a completely different subset that may even include facilities at other hotel chains.

True fixed networks have been built by many companies, including Merrill Lynch, Hewlett-Packard, Sears, J. C. Penney, General Motors and others because of their need to transmit to the same sites over and over again. Most of these fixed networks are private and not available to outsiders for videoconference use.

WHEN IS VIDEOCONFERENCING APPROPRIATE?

As a rule, though, the companies that have installed permanent networks continue to follow a series of steps similar to those needed for ad hoc videoconferencing. These steps, in fact, were often refined by these companies during their experimentation with ad hoc events that preceded their decisions to build private networks.

Susan J. Irwin of Irwin Communications, a Washington-based consulting firm, has worked in the satellite field for over 10 years and helps companies determine when the time is right for them to install a private network. Irwin says that, although several factors come into play in making such a decision, cost justification is usually the first to be considered. In most cases, she says, the justification is there if the company is holding at least two large ad hoc events per year, that is, events that use about 100 receive sites.

In justifying a permanent network the first step is to analyze the same costs that occur in an ad hoc event (see Chapter 3). However, other considerations are just as important in considering a permanent installation. Irwin says that the following questions should be asked to help determine the feasibility—and the real need—for a fixed network:

- How much communication goes from the company's headquarters to remote locations?
- How much of that communication would be enhanced by live video?
- How much training is being done by the company?
- How much travel is involved between headquarters and the remote locations?

Irwin emphasizes that the most obvious and practical use of fixed videoconferencing networks is in training. Companies are using their facilities to train their own employees as well as customers. For example, MicroAge, a chain of computer stores, is installing a fixed network to teach its customers about its products. This not only results in customers being better able to use the equipment and software purchased at MicroAge, it gets them back into the store as they attend the satellite-delivered training programs.

Apart from cost justification issues, adds Irwin, the type of company that could benefit most from a permanent network will probably have a profile that includes many of the following characteristics:

- a large organization that is geographically dispersed
- a centralized headquarters
- a business that is sales- or service-driven
- the need for timely information
- a competitive environment
- a large training or education requirement
- past experience either with taped video programs or ad hoc videoconference productions

Irwin says that the list of industry types that have already begun to use permanent networks widely—insurance, banking and brokerage, retail, franchising, automobiles, health care—reflect the profile outlined above. Irwin emphasizes, however, that the success of any network depends on its ability to perform an important communications function for the company: "The existence of technology is useless without a lot of emphasis on what it is used for."

There are also other, more peripheral, benefits to owning a private network. Once a network is in place and tested, the networking process itself usually becomes standardized, and individual events become relatively easy to produce. This is particularly true if a company hires a systems integrator such as Private Satellite Network or VideoStar Connections to handle the technical functions of transmission and network monitoring.

Another interesting option open to many of those with permanent networks is cross-networking. Irwin describes this as the controlled ability for one private network owner to access a network belonging to another company, for example, a supplier or a customer. Texas Instruments has repeatedly used its private network capability to communicate productively with Hewlett-Packard, one of its customers.

Ad hoc videoconferencing gives an organization that may be considering the installation of a private network the opportunity to use satellite communications on a temporary basis, allowing it to try out the medium without the burden of a long-term financial commitment.

You may be excited by the possibilities that satellite communications can offer you. Your reaction is certainly justified by the reality of the many successful videoconferencing events that have taken place (see Chapter 2). However, before you proceed to present the idea to management, there are some things that need careful consideration.

First is the cost of videoconferencing. Chapter 3 covers the details involved in justifying a videoconference project. But in a nutshell, videoconferencing can be expensive, with projects starting at about $20,000 and climbing to a quarter of a million dollars or more. Whether this is truly too expensive, in the context of other projects done within your organization, only you and your management can tell.

Second is the capability of the videoconference medium to meet your communications needs effectively. Gerry Hendrixson, of Procter & Gamble (P&G) Company's Photo/Graphics Department, has been responsible for the production of several videoconferences at that company. Hendrixson says that P&G now has a set of criteria for evaluating whether a videoconference is appropriate in any given case. He asks the manager interested in videoconferencing a series of questions:

1. Are you trying to reach an audience of 100 or more persons?
2. Is this audience widely scattered among a number of geographic locations?
3. Is it important that the message be received at all locations simultaneously?
4. Do you want everyone in the audience to receive exactly the same message in the same way?
5. Do you expect the audience to interact with the presenters?

If yes is the answer to four of the five questions, a satellite meeting is seriously considered.

Hendrixson also points out that the greatest overall weight that tips the scale in favor of a videoconference is the cost savings. He says that P&G considers the cost of a traditional meeting (and it has a great deal of meeting history on which to draw). The planners include in the calculation not only out-of-pocket costs but the value of the employees' time spent in travel to a centralized meeting.

The idea of videoconferencing is now well accepted at P&G and established procedures are in place for ordering a videoconference. First, management asks for an estimate of cost and a timetable required to complete the project. Quotes are gathered on services. A vendor is selected, and the whole process is turned over to the buying department for contracting.

This acceptance at P&G was hard-won. It took quite a while to convince management to try its first videoconference (for the introduction of Liquid Ivory hand soap). Hendrixson's department, which normally provides services to the rest of P&G on a cross-chargeable basis, gave a special price to this first client. The lower price was looked at as a trade-off that allowed the Photo/Graphics Department to enhance the education of its own personnel. Hendrixson says that this incentive was put in place for the first user because "we believed it could be done. We believed it could be effective." Repeated use of videoconferencing has since proved him right.

Len Aulenbach, audiovisual manager at Smith Kline & French Laboratories, related the considerations that convinced him to produce his first videoconference for his company. He wanted to communicate a uniform message in a timely manner. He knew that he had something unusual to communicate (a restructuring of the sales force), and he wanted the message to stand out as important.

Aulenbach says that costs also played an important role in his recommendation for a videoconference. He examined the funds already set aside for regularly scheduled sales promotion meetings. There was a budget for those meetings, and happily, Aulenbach found that the videoconference he had planned was "significantly less expensive" than the centralized national meetings they had held in the past. "No matter what we did with the videoconference, it would be less expensive than a national meeting." Now, Aulenbach says, videoconferences are included as a part of their regular budget. (See Figure 1.3.)

Kip Knight, a brand manager at P&G, who was involved

Figure 1.3: Smith Kline & French Laboratories executive panel conferring before answering a question during a videoconference. Photo courtesy SmithKline Beckman.

with its first videoconference and who has since used the medium for other products, is sold on the benefits of satellite communications. Knight, who remembers road trips that took weeks to get product announcements to the field, likes the relative speed of communicating a message through satellite transmission. He cites the possibility of a "quick response to competition." He also likes the live, up-to-the-minute nature of the medium. "If anything has changed [in the business] we know about it [when we go on air]." This means that the latest information is available to everyone simultaneously.

Knight stresses the importance of being able to reach more people deeper within the organization through videoconferencing. "[You're] better off getting the message to everybody. The guy pounding the pavement will make the difference. You can reach him with a videoconference." Knight, who has been on screen as videoconference talent, mentions one other benefit that he considers a real plus. "When I go out to the field, I don't have to introduce myself. They know who I am."

This visibility may be important to future generations of management as they hope to achieve success within large organizations. Putting in a credible appearance in a videoconference gives a person a degree of exposure to others within the corporation that would not otherwise be possible. These days, we can't deny the value of making the most of a TV appearance—as illustrated by Lee Iacocca, Victor Kiam and every U.S. president elected within the past 20 years.

This book will help you bring these benefits to your company. Don't be afraid to take on the challenge of a videoconference. Follow the suggestions in this book, ask for help when you need it and plan a first event that you think is manageable with the staff available to you.

SUMMARY

Videoconferencing has been made possible by the development of satellite communications systems that provide a means to transmit a television signal inexpensively and efficiently. Satellites circle the earth in geostationary orbits above the equator, making access to them possible in every part of the globe. Most users have found that while it may have been difficult to convince management to try satellite communications the first time, once tried, videoconferencing has been accepted enthusiastically as an effective part of the communications mix.

2

Identifying Applications

The sky is quite literally the limit in videoconferencing. Every day, it seems, someone comes up with yet another creative way to use the medium. Still, for most of us who must present a clear explanation of the medium and suggestions for practical use to company management, it helps to have an understanding of how others have used it. There's no point in reinventing the wheel. This chapter is meant to help you pick up the wheel where the inventor left it and use it to your company's best advantage.

Within the framework of decision criteria discussed in Chapter 1 (dispersed audience, large audience, etc.) there are many likely uses for videoconferencing:

- sales meetings, assuming that salespeople are widely scattered throughout the United States or the world
- product introductions, at which videoconferencing makes it possible to launch a product simultaneously to everyone with a need to know
- pay-per-view events, for which attendees pay an admission fee at the door to participate, and which often involve teaching, with satellite delivery making the best teachers available to all
- speaker delivery, allowing a sought-after presenter to appear in numerous locations without leaving town or disrupting anyone's schedule
- fundraising, which takes the TV telethon idea into the realm of privately configured networks.

WHO'S USING VIDEOCONFERENCING

The applications outlined above fall into obvious user niches. For example, satellite-delivered sales meetings are usually held by large companies and fundraisers are usually held by nonprofit groups. The statistics on who uses videoconferences show a shift from the nonprofit into the profit sector. Ten or so years ago, when the Public Service Satellite Consortium was first introducing the idea of satellite usage for meetings, the majority of users were educational institutions and government agencies, with the total number of projects being small enough to be reckoned on the fingers of one hand.

More recent statistics, compiled between January 1984 and October 1985 by the Center for Interactive Programs at the University of Wisconsin-Extension in Madison, showed that 227 ad hoc videoconferences were reported as being held during that time, with 52% of them sponsored by corporations, 34% by associations and the remainder split between education and government. Of course, many videoconferences are not reported and fail to show up in the statistics.

To get an idea of the general types of applications that were most prevalent among users, the survey divided videoconferences into three categories: those that were designed (1) to disseminate business information such as an annual report to shareholders, (2) for educational or training uses and (3) for sales or marketing conferences (such as new product demonstrations).

The survey showed that 46.7% of the videoconferences were produced for business information purposes, 34.8% for education and training and 18.5% for sales and marketing. These results clearly show heavy business usage. This change to corporate clients has opened up the medium to more creative uses in a setting where this creativity can be afforded.

Corporate Users

Corporations typically use videoconferences for sales meetings, product introductions, training and an occasional press conference. The list of companies using videoconferencing includes many of the best-known names in the *Fortune* 500. Several have been selected as representative of corporate usage.

Since the beginning of videoconferencing the automakers have seen the advantages of satellite communications and have profited from it. Ford, General Motors and Chrysler have all been regular users, with other auto companies employing the medium occasionally for special events.

Judy Masserang, manager of Video Systems Support at Electronic Data Systems Corp. (EDS) and formerly manager of WTVS Detroit's videoconferencing subsidiary Vision Communications, has worked with all three of the largest auto companies in videoconferencing. Masserang points to the tremendous feeling of corporate unity that can result from videoconferencing, especially since the medium can give personnel at plant sites the opportunity to see and to interact with top management—people whom they would never meet in any other way.

Ford has made good use of videoconferencing to introduce new models to its dealers and the press. In January 1985 Ford showed off prototypes of the new Ford Taurus and Mercury Sable at a Los Angeles press conference that was transmitted live by satellite to district sales offices across the nation. The conference featured a presentation by Chairman Phillip Caldwell, who was to retire a few days following the broadcast.

In February 1986 Ford introduced its Merkur Scorpio to representatives of the U.S. news media, who attended the videoconference at the Chicago Automobile Show. The broadcast originated from Ford's design studio near Cologne, West Germany.

Chrysler Corporation has made such frequent use of videoconferencing that in 1982 it decided to install its own network at its district offices. Chrysler had quite a bit of experience with videoconferencing before taking that step. It had broadcast every week for almost a year to alternating audiences of sales and service people with programs ranging from pep talks (the broadcasts began when Chrysler's fortunes seemed at their lowest ebb) to training. These were generally shirtsleeve working sessions done in the simplest possible setting with a great deal of live voice interaction from the remote sites.

General Motors has also installed its own network; in fact, it has two. One is for Chevrolet and one for Pontiac. Uses at General Motors vary, but one innovation was the video discus-

Figure 2.1: Talent rehearsing in the studio before a satellite introduction of Spic and Span Liquid Pine. The set featured a live pine forest. Photo courtesy The Procter & Gamble Company.

sion between plant personnel directors and GM executives of an agreement with the United Auto Workers even before the agreement was to be voted upon by the UAW membership.

Procter & Gamble (P&G), the giant consumer products company, uses ad hoc videoconferencing in two principal ways: to announce product innovations to the press and to introduce new products—both Liquid Ivory hand soap and Spic and Span Pine Cleaner—to their salespeople throughout the United States, as shown in Figure 2.1.

The idea behind P&G's satellite product introductions is to disseminate information simultaneously to everyone who has a need to know. The added benefit is that it replaces the "dog and pony" road shows that had been a more typical approach for the company. P&G has also used the medium for sales meetings to help avoid the cost in time and money involved in setting up centralized meetings at its Cincinnati headquarters.

P&G's videoconferences have ranged from bare-bones in-studio productions to more highly polished presentations, one of which originated from its new headquarters, opening with a pre-produced tape featuring employees singing on the square outside the building. Camera shots were taken from a hovering helicopter.

SmithKline Beckman's Smith Kline & French Laboratories has also used videoconferencing for internal purposes. When its sales force was reorganized in 1986, sales representatives learned firsthand about the changes via satellite. SmithKline opted to use a videoconference when it realized there was no time to organize a centralized meeting at its Philadelphia headquarters. Management chose a simple in-studio setting with a live audience that made the presentation process more natural and comfortable for all concerned.

Pay-Per-View

When pay-per-view is mentioned, most people think of prizefights delivered by satellite. That's the right idea, but others have taken the concept and used it to distribute information. The main users of pay-per-view in this context are associations that recoup their videoconference costs through attendance fees paid at the door or in advance. This technique has made videoconferencing possible for several groups that could not otherwise have afforded it.

The American Home Sewing Association, for instance, charges a fee for home economists and others interested in sewing to attend a videoconference, generally once a year, that updates the viewers on the latest techniques in home sewing. The National Dairy Council uses pay-per-view to deliver training on nutrition to professional dieticians. Its first session, on the importance of calcium, drew large crowds at 50 sites.

The Mechanical Contractors Association of America has held many successful educational pay-per-views that, according to their former director of education, Dick Maresco, have not only paid for themselves but have made money for the association. (For more about the financing of pay-per-views, see Chapter 3.)

The American Law Institute and the American Bar Association have been so pleased with the response to their pay-per-views aimed at the law community that they now own their own network and transmit training programs about every other week.

The key to a successful pay-per-view, says Dick Maresco, now director of management education at Associated Builders and Contractors in Washington, DC is to identify a real need and "make sure it's got a large enough umbrella to bring in the money."

Speaker Delivery

Making a sought-after speaker available to a wide audience is a side benefit in many videoconferences. Occasionally, however, a videoconference is set up for the sole purpose of delivering a speaker. This can be especially beneficial to groups located in cities that are rarely visited by top-name speakers.

A prime example is Buena Vista College in Storm Lake, Iowa. Buena Vista is a small, progressive college in the northwest corner of Iowa. When it was time to dedicate a new telecommunications center in May of 1985, President Keith Briscoe—realizing that his school was not on the beaten tour path—arranged to have a keynote speaker's address arrive by satellite. The result was a highly successful dedication with a well-received speech by a Texas Instruments executive, live from Dallas.

Later in that same year, Briscoe wanted to honor a Buena Vista benefactor. He had hoped to have one of the state's U.S. senators make the presentation, but the senator was in Washington, unable to travel to Iowa for the function. The solution was a videoconference with live, televised give-and-take between the honoree and the senator that surprised the donor during a testimonial dinner.

Fund-Raising

Raising money is never an easy task, but the road to contributions is smoothed when the audience is made up of your group's supporters, who can attend right in their hometowns.

The University of Illinois has been remarkably successful at using videoconferencing during a fund-raising campaign. In April 1984, nearing the end of a five-year effort to raise $100 million, the university held a videoconference to encourage supporters to push hard during the last few months of the campaign to make the goal a reality.

To create excitement and a feeling of unity among key alumni, the university transmitted live video and audio broadcasts from five cities. It featured famous Illinois alumni such as John Chancellor of NBC News and retired General Motors Chairman Thomas Murphy. The broadcast reached 4000 alumni in 19 cities.

The productive uses to which people have put videoconferencing could fill this book and more. The important thing is to know when a videoconference is appropriate. Don't assume that just because your program is being delivered via outer space that that alone will make it special—it won't. EDS's Judy Masserang uses a good rule of thumb: "The message must surpass the medium."

SUMMARY

The uses of videoconferencing are widely varied. The only limitations are your imagination and your ability to finance the project. Corporations that hold internal meetings and product introductions by satellite are now the largest users of the medium. They are followed by trade and professional associations, which use the medium mainly to deliver pay-per-view educational programs to their members.

3

Justifying the Cost

"What does it cost?" is usually the first question I hear from someone who is considering the use of videoconferencing. Although there is no simple answer to that question, because the components can vary so widely, some guidelines are in order. In this chapter you'll learn how to approach the task of cost justification, the importance of including expenses that are not obvious out-of-pocket costs and the major objections you are likely to hear regarding the cost of videoconferencing.

BUDGETING THE VIDEOCONFERENCE

First, a real budget (see Table 3.1). The budget summary that appears here is intentionally placed at the beginning of the chapter to help you see why cost justification is important. Videoconferencing is expensive—maybe not when compared with its logical alternatives—but costly nevertheless.

This budget is taken from a project completed recently. The videoconference to which it relates was two hours long, with a two-hour system test. There were 21 receive sites, each seating an average of 50 people. The receive sites were high-quality hotels. The production itself took place in an established television studio.

Studio time was used for two days prior to the event for set preparation, talent rehearsals and preparation of graphic materials to be incorporated into the videoconference. The entire production was shot live before a small studio audience.

The most elusive variable in a budget like this is the produc-

Table 3.1: A 21-Site Videoconference Budget

TRANSMISSION (includes uplinking, satellite time and insurance coverage)	$ 4,175
PRODUCTION (includes in-studio production, all equipment for a three-camera shoot, crew, teleprompter preparation, rehearsal, set preparation, production of electronic graphics, pre-production consultation sessions)	18,000
RECEIVE SITES (includes the following services at each of 21 high-quality hotels: downlinks, downlink technicians, large-screen video equipment, backup audiovisual equipment, audiovisual technicians, audio equipment, hotel meeting rooms, preparation of site facilitators' guide, phone in room for question-and-answer session)	37,415
PROFESSIONAL PROJECT MANAGEMENT	26,250
TOTAL	$85,840

tion portion. A videoconference production can cost anywhere from $5000 to the sky. We will examine the costs involved in production in greater detail in Chapter 5.

The next most elusive variables are the costs at the receive sites. This varies throughout the United States. But in general, if you're paying a fee somewhere in the price range listed below, you're doing all right:

- $750 to $850 per eight-hour day for a downlink and technician
- $500 to $1000 per day for large-screen audiovisual equipment with equivalent backup; small screens (19" to 25") are just not adequate, even for backup
- $20 to $25 per hour for an audiovisual technician to stay at the site beyond setup, to be on hand in case of trouble
- $75 to $300 or more for a hotel meeting room to seat 50 or so people. This item will vary with the quality of the hotel, the kind of food service required and local market conditions

Now that you have seen these numbers you probably understand why it is important to be able to justify this type of event. Of course, management everywhere must be cautious about expenditures of all types. But when the expenditure is in five or six figures for a service that your manager may not understand very well, the justification becomes even more important.

One word of caution: In many cases videoconferencing of any stripe is just not cost-justifiable. Be aware of that. Unless you have a real need to access many people in many locations simultaneously, you will probably not be able to justify the cost. On the other hand, the larger your audience and the more cities you need to reach, the easier it is to justify.

COST COMPARISON

Do your homework before presenting your manager with your cost figures. Identify the alternative communication methods you could use and how much they would cost. In most cases a videoconference is replacing some type of meeting, for example, a national sales meeting. If your company has held national sales meetings in the past, find out how much they have cost.

Kip Knight, Procter & Gamble brand manager, has used videoconferencing on many occasions. He thoroughly compares the costs of a videoconference to those of more traditional events before deciding which way to deliver any meeting.

Knight sees the videoconference as usually easy to justify, once all the comparison data are in, because "a lot of people don't appreciate how much it costs to have a [traditional] sales meeting. It involves time, transportation, housing, feeding, plus the cost of putting on the show."

Knight's pricing comparison includes (a) the costs of doing the same general types of meetings in the past, (b) the budget set for this particular meeting and (c) the time estimated to prepare and complete the meeting.

Knight is especially convinced that the road show of old is the most logical candidate for replacement by videoconferencing. He says that before videoconferencing was available, a typical new product was introduced to employees on the road. Five or more people (three operators and two management talents) would have to travel to a dozen or more cities. This could take months. A videoconference takes only a few weeks to prepare and complete, so there is a substantial saving in valuable employee time. Further, Knight says there's an advantage of timing:

"The fastest we could do a road show is two months because of setup and teardown. If speed of attack is important, a videoconference has the advantage."

All of these factors are quantifiable, even the time lag. Sales may be lost in the West because only the salespeople in the East have the new product information.

You may have to dig into many budgets to get this information. In most organizations the costs have come from several budgets. The sales department may have kicked in a few thousand dollars, public relations may have contributed a bit, research may have provided some dollars and so on. That's one reason just quoting the cost of a videoconference doesn't work—even if you know that the videoconference represents a tremendous saving. The odds are that the one manager who will see the videoconference estimate knows only what his or her department contributed and really has no idea what a complete meeting costs. That manager will need documentation if you are going to make your justification believable.

Something else to keep in mind as you look at comparative meeting costs is the value of management time. Look at the last big traditional meeting you had. Who managed it? How much money does that person make in salary and benefits? Add that to the total cost for your comparison. Be aware, though, in doing your thorough evaluation, that time will also be needed to manage the videoconference. In fact, more may be needed for the first event.

Probably the greatest single economy is related to time saved by employees attending the event. Are they sales reps? How much do they make per average hour in salary or commissions? How much, then, do they lose for the company when they're spending their time traveling to a traditional meeting instead of selling a customer?

You also need to be aware of the hot buttons of your management. If your company has a great deal of money to spend on meetings with an upper management that loves the "touchy-feely" approach, forget it. The chances of your getting a videoconference approved are nil. The most likely user of videoconferencing will be a company that recognizes the need for communication, is interested in keeping down costs and is willing to use a high-tech approach for at least some meetings. (See Figure 3.1.)

HOW ONE COMPANY JUSTIFIED ITS VIDEOCONFERENCE

One company with which I have worked developed a justification technique that may be adopted by others. The company was about to introduce a new product and wanted an innovative way to present it to an audience of potential clients. The planners decided to use videoconferencing for a simultaneous approach call—using their best salesman, the company president, to call on all customers at once to introduce the product, thus paving the way for local reps to close sales in the following weeks. This company's executives knew from experience that no order would be taken on that first call since the product they were introducing was a costly item. They also thought they would increase their chances of gaining the ears of their prospects with a presentation from their president.

Even though this idea met with instant approval in principle, it was necessary to justify the costs involved as compared with other, more traditional, methods of product introduction. So they examined two main items that they decided were pertinent to the introduction and sales of a new product. They were (1) the cost per field sales call and (2) the average gross revenues per salesperson per day. Here's how they figured their costs:

1. Their average cost per sales call was $125. If they included a total of 1000 clients in a one-day satellite approach call, the value of that call would be equal to $125,000 in traditional calls. (Since they had only 50 sales reps, it would have taken them seven days to call on these clients instead of the one videoconference day.)
2. Their average salesperson grossed $2 million per year in sales, or about $8439 per day. Considering that their selling year had 237 days, this meant that their 50 salespeople grossed an average of $421,941 per day.

In the past they had introduced new products to sales reps by bringing them together at one central site for a meeting. But

Figure 3.1: A panel of executives responding to questions during a videoconference originating on location at Procter & Gamble headquarters. Photo courtesy The Procter & Gamble Company.

that took salespeople out of the field for two or three days of travel time. The new method, videoconferencing, reduced the number of lost selling days to one.

Thus, the decision was easy since the price of a day of sales calls ($125,000)—which would have been spent in any case—plus the value in gross volume of even one lost sales day ($421,941) added up to $546,941 and the cost of the videoconference was to be $150,000.

Appendix B at the end of this book contains a cost justification worksheet that they developed. You can use it to see if their method works for you.

Of course, in most cases, you will compare the cost of a videoconference with the more direct costs of typical meetings. Here is how another company did that.

The planners were considering holding a four-hour meeting by satellite and wanted to compare that to their past experiences flying 500 employees from 20 different cities to one site for a traditional conference. Table 3.2 shows their comparative budgets.

OVERCOMING OBJECTIONS

Videoconferencing is a radically new technology for most people. For that reason, even though you have done your homework on cost justification, you may find objections that are not

Table 3.2: Comparative Costs of a Videoconference and Face-to-Face Meeting

VIDEOCONFERENCE		TRADITIONAL MEETING	
Videoconference package	$90,000		
		Air fares @ $200 × 500 attendees	$100,000
		Hotel @ $75 × 500	37,500
		Meals @ $50 × 500	25,000
Auto travel to		Ground transportation @ $8 × 500	4,000
videoconference sites	2,000	Ballroom rental	1,000
Total	$92,000	Total	$167,500
Cost per person	$184	Cost per person	$335

based on finances. New technology is scary for many people, and simple dollar savings will not be enough to turn the trick. Certain objections are likely to be heard:

- "Videoconferencing costs too much." This is where you trot out your justification homework.
- "We don't have the staff time to pull off something so complicated." You should have figures to show how much staff time is involved in the traditional approach. Be prepared, though, to acknowledge that your staff will spend about one person-day per site to prepare for the typical videoconference.
- "We can't risk so much money on an unproven technology." The technology has been around for over a decade. Be prepared with names of companies, and contacts at those companies, that have videoconferenced successfully.
- "It only cost me $——— for our last sales meeting." Ask if your manager has included funds that other departments may have chipped in.
- "I don't like this high-tech stuff. I'd rather meet with the troops in person on their own turf." That may be fine on occasion, but ask your manager to figure out the value of his or her own time. Is it economical to be out of the office for days on end visiting branch offices?

Some objections, of course, are merely convenient excuses to avoid the stress of trying something new. So this time you may not get to try your videoconference. Keep at it. As your management notices other companies making good use of the technology, it will see the light. And you will be prepared.

SOURCES OF DOLLARS

So far we have looked at videoconference expenditures from the standpoint of a company that will foot the entire bill on its own, usually out of pre-established marketing, public relations or other meeting budgets. However, there are other ways to finance a videoconference.

Charging a Fee

Associations often charge fees. Examine the distribution of likely attendees throughout the United States. Figure out the most logical network of cities that could accommodate the bulk of these attendees. Then figure the cost of producing and distributing a videoconference to these people in these cities. Divide the videoconference cost by a conservative estimate of the number of likely attendees, and *voilà!* you have your admission price. If you want to make this a fund-raising venture, add a few dollars to the price of admission. Be very careful, though, to price the event high enough to cover your costs and keep yourself out of the red afterward.

Dick Maresco, director of management education at Associated Builders and Contractors, has had a great deal of experience and success in financing videoconferences this way. He points out that the biggest reason money is more often lost than made at pay-per-view events is that the user "usually doesn't do a good job defining his program. The vendor proposals are no good because the user left out some of his needs." And last-minute additions to a program can cause alarming increases in price. (For a full discussion of production pricing see Chapter 5.)

Maresco says he cuts his risk by bearing no financial responsibility for the receive sites. He has local association chapters agree to sponsor them. The local chapter pays a fee to Maresco's group at the home office. The chapter, in turn, sets a fee for local participants (usually about $100 per person) that is high enough to produce some income.

Caroline Laden, director of the American Law Network, which delivers training to attorneys via a fixed satellite network, takes a slightly different approach. Individuals pay their fees (about $120 for a four-hour session, with workbooks, followed by local discussions) directly to the network office in Philadelphia. Production costs are paid out of these fees, and proceeds left over are shared by the network and the organization that sponsored the videoconference.

Keep in mind that this type of pay-per-view event will have some costs associated with it not incurred by most internal corporate events.

Publicity Costs

Only you know your group well enough to determine how to sell to its members, but in most cases you should count on printing and mailing announcement materials. Perhaps you will also need to place some ads in appropriate trade publications.

Maresco's group helps the local chapters market the program by sending out several weeks in advance (1) a complete marketing package with ad slicks, (2) recommended press releases and (3) a large quantity of printed brochures.

The home office also does a direct mailing to individual members announcing the event.

In addition, Maresco recommends that the local chapter hire temporary help to phone all members, encouraging them to come and bring guests. He thinks this is especially important for a chapter's first event.

Caroline Laden says that it takes a full year to market one of her group's pay-per-view programs. The American Law Network uses contacts in local markets to sell event attendance. Detailed descriptions of the event are provided to the local market 120 to 150 days in advance of the air date to allow enough time to print a brochure and ensure adequate attendance.

Site Facilitator Cost

In a typical corporate event, an employee acts as host or hostess at each receive site. At many pay-per-view events, a professional host is hired as well as people to take paid admissions at the door. Firms that specialize in temporary personnel usually have the kind of people required to do this work. They must usually be hired market by market, adding to your administrative costs as well as the cost of the personnel themselves.

Acquiring Sponsorship

If your videoconference is certain to access a large audience, you may be able to get sponsorship of the event from companies associated with your industry. If you are affiliated with an educational institution, you may be able to get sponsor support from foundations, government agencies or businesses sympathetic to the message you will be delivering.

Increasing Membership Dues

Suppose you would like to deliver training to your members on a regular basis via satellite. Increase your dues to cover the cost. Once your members understand that a small increase in dues will replace large expenditures in travel to seminar sites, they should readily agree.

SUMMARY

Videoconferences, like anything else, can be sold only on the basis of perceived value. The first videoconference will be the hardest to justify. Do your financial homework before suggesting the idea to your manager. Once you have done one and your financial cost-effectiveness projections have come true, selling the second one should be easy.

Above all, don't be crestfallen if your most convincing arguments fail to persuade the first time. Keep at it. Every new idea takes a long time to be adopted into a culture—even the most progressive corporate culture. As long as your justification is real—not just a set of numbers to give you the chance to play with a new toy—you'll eventually win the day.

4

Planning and Preparation

Considerable planning must take place before the networking begins, the studio is booked and the scriptwriters start work. A videoconference—even in its simplest form—is a complicated project that interrelates people (and their personalities) with technology (and its quirks). Only with careful planning can a project of this nature be successful.

The objective of all this planning is to place yourself in a position of understanding your project thoroughly. You should know all the elements of it intimately. You should know clearly what is to be accomplished. Without this you will probably waste a great deal of money and a lot of time (which is money) on production changes, and you may suffer an assortment of unpleasant surprises.

You will be responsible for coordinating the efforts of many people in many cities. (See Chapter 9 for a full discussion of project management techniques.) You will never meet most of these people and therefore you will never get to understand their working idiosyncrasies. The plan you will implement must make it possible for you and them to work together so that each can understand the wishes and objectives of the other.

Videoconferences can look simple, but as in all television production, preparation is essential. Clarence (Clare) Mann, a Cincinnati producer who has worked on major videoconference projects with Procter & Gamble, SmithKline Beckman and others, says that a videoconference is produced just the same as any other television show, "whether it's five minutes or five hours, everything is important. You don't just turn it on and it works."

Given this level of complexity in even a simple production, a bit of advice from Caroline Laden, director of the American Law Network, is in order. Directing her remarks toward the first-time videoconference user in particular, she warns that a project should not be made more complicated than necessary. "The detail is enormous," she says. "You just can't keep all those threads going."

Judy Masserang of EDS considers planning so important that she has developed a document that she sends her clients at General Motors while they are still in the earliest phases of considering videoconferencing. A copy of her "Broadcast Checklist" is included in the appendix.

One further suggestion before putting your pen to paper to fill out Masserang's form. Watch someone else's videoconference before you plan your own. Lee Ferguson, Procter & Gamble's internal videoconference producer, says, "Watch one happen. See how it falls together." Once you've done that and have reconciled yourself to a methodical planning process, you will be ready to begin.

THE FIRST PLANNING MEETING

The first step is to set up a preliminary meeting of all those who will be involved in the videoconference. You probably will decide not to include any outside vendors at this meeting. You need an opportunity to examine the situation and assess your own in-house capabilities without the pressure of hearing a sales pitch. Later on, once you are beyond this stage, those vendors will be useful. But by that time, you will be better prepared to get from them what you really need—not what they want you to hear.

Who should attend? Anyone who you think could be helpful. For example:

- the manager responsible for the program
- the talent (if identified and available)
- an in-house public relations person
- an in-house advertising professional
- in-house TV production personnel, if any

- in-house audiovisual personnel
- in-house writers
- an in-house meeting planner
- a recording secretary

You may not need all these people on your project. On the other hand, you may need more or different people. But this list includes people with expertise in communications who may, at least, offer some excellent suggestions in this early phase.

By the way, this meeting should be taking place as far in advance of the project as possible. If it is to be a pay-per-view that will need to be marketed, you should hold your first meeting a year in advance. If it is an internal, U.S.–only videoconference, try to be at this point three months before air date. If overseas locations will be part of your network, give yourself six months. Don't panic, though, if you have already made your decision and time is running short. You will just have to work harder and smarter to get it all done. These time suggestions are the ideal, but since when do we live in an ideal world?

At this first meeting you will not get answers to all your questions. Be prepared, however, to ask all the important questions so that the answers can be ready for meeting number two.

Question Outline for First Meeting

1. *What is the purpose of the videoconference?* The manager responsible for deciding to do a videoconference should have the answer to that—whether to introduce a new product, hold a sales meeting, etc.
2. *Why has a videoconference been chosen over other possible meeting types?* The answer to this question will give you some insight into how to proceed. For example, if the answer is to save money, you should be planning on a simple production. If the answer is to wow 'em out in the field, you should awaken your sleeping creativity and go for it (translated as "a big budget is in order").
3. *Who is the intended audience?* The answer to this will

also help point you in the appropriate direction for your production. Sixty-year-old New York investment bankers will probably not respond as well to a program that could excite and motivate 21-year-old sales recruits. Keep this simple fact in front of you at all times. You are putting on the show for the audience—not for yourself.

4. *What date has been chosen for broadcast?* Use this as the date from which to work backwards as you develop the timetable for your project. (See Chapter 9.)

5. *Will the videoconference be part of some larger, more inclusive program dependent on departments outside your control?* This will identify flags for you. For example, will the actual air date depend upon the timely production of a sales kit? Will you need to coordinate visuals to match a workbook or other materials? Is there a definite theme you will need to follow? What is the likelihood of the departments responsible for these tasks completing their jobs on time for the videoconference? What control will you be given over their efforts?

6. *Whose idea was the project?* This will help you understand the project better if internal politics are a consideration at your place of business.

7. *Who will the speakers be? Where will they be coming from? Is their availability limited?*

8. *Who is writing the script?*

9. *How soon can the script be finished, and who must approve it?*

10. *What mood are you trying to project?* Is this a somber announcement or a joyous occasion? Do you want to project a casual or a formal image?

11. *Is the content of the broadcast sensitive enough to warrant scrambling?*

12. *Do materials already exist that could be incorporated into the videoconference so that time and money can be saved?* Most companies have something useful—perhaps slides or videotape of the office or of people at work.

13. *Should the broadcast originate in a studio or at some other location?*

14. *How many receive sites will be in the network?*
15. *What kinds of receive sites are desired?*
16. *How many people will attend at each site?*
17. *Will food or beverages be associated with the videoconference?*
18. *Will sleeping rooms at the receive sites be necessary?*
19. *Will the meetings extend beyond the videoconference so that additional breakout rooms or audiovisual equipment will be needed at the remote sites?*
20. *Is the event to be pay-per-view?* This will prompt the need to consider the tasks related to selling the program to outsiders.

Some of these questions may not be answered at the first meeting. Set a definite date for the second meeting, with the understanding that all answers will be gathered in the meantime.

Follow-Up

Between meetings, do your own homework. Now that you have a feel for the scope of the project, examine possible origination sites. Get an idea of what types of production facilities are available and ask for (and check out) their references. If you've done this before the next meeting, you'll be all set to begin the project once all the questions have been resolved. This can be of great importance if you are working under a tight time schedule.

Talk to the person in charge of looking for usable pre-existing materials. Use a slide viewer such as the Diastar 200 (available in most audiovisual supply stores) to look at each slide to be sure that it meets the aspect ratio necessary for TV. You don't want to discover too late that important information is hanging over the edge of the television screen, out of sight of the audience.

If the speaking talent has been selected, meet with them for an informal discussion. Find out how much experience they have had in front of a camera to determine if you will need some outside assistance in coaching them. Above all, "Make the talent aware that you're trying to make them look good," advises Gerry Hendrixson of Procter & Gamble's Photo/Graphics Department. The success of the program will depend largely upon the positive attitude—or reluctance—of the talent. If they understand that you are on their side, you will be one leg up toward a successful production.

Meet with the scriptwriters to get an accurate assessment of how soon you can expect finished scripts. You will not be able to proceed very far with the program until you have the scripts, so the timing here may establish the entire schedule for the project. Gerry Hendrixson says that you should emphasize that you need plenty of time "to visually support the scripts in an interesting way." Without the scripts you will not know how long the finished program will be, what graphics you should use or what supporting materials have yet to be produced.

THE SECOND MEETING

Invite all those who attended the first meeting and anyone else who will have a role in the videoconference.

Review answers to the questions already posed. Take up any new questions that may have arisen.

The purpose of this meeting will be to gather enough information to outline the tasks required to complete the project and to assign people to those tasks. (More on project management in Chapter 9.)

Examine each task to determine which member of the organization would be best suited to handle it—either through experience or inclination. Your motivation here is to determine whether you should hand full responsibility for certain tasks to an insider or whether you should hire an outside vendor.

If you come to the conclusion that you would like an outside vendor to work on the project, decide exactly what you would like that vendor to do. Most vendors prefer to do a turnkey videoconference project. This gives them control over the project and also earns them the most money. However, most vendors are willing to provide just the parts of the videoconference that you cannot handle on your own.

Assuming that you have the employee time to spare, you may be well advised to involve your own people to give them exposure to the videoconferencing medium. Even though this will take more of your supervision, this effort can be a good investment if future videoconferences are anticipated. In many cases an organization has employees capable of handling videoconference details with, at most, a little outside consulting help. Here are the major tasks that will need to be accomplished.

Television Production

This is the task that most people must hire out. If you have your own in-house production team, great! Use it. But if your in-house expertise is limited to highly edited videotape or slide shows, don't use it. Live television, which is what videoconferencing is, is a completely different art form.

Scriptwriting

Even though you may need an outsider to polish the script, no one is better equipped to write about new products, sales or other company business than your own employees. If you hire an outsider to write the script from scratch, the delays can be interminable as the writer gets up to speed on the language of your product. If you are like most companies, you have insider jokes and jargon that no outsider could ever hope to incorporate in the program, and the results could end up being very dry and impersonal.

Networking and Transmission

Ordering and managing these services is where you may have been inclined—before reading this book—to call on the help of an outsider. The questions you need to ask as you speak with technicians to order services at the receive sites are discussed in later chapters. These technicians represent an ever-changing industry. New companies are being formed and old ones closing almost daily. There are published guides, though, to set you on the path of contacting the correct people. These are listed in the Bibliography at the end of this book. The important thing to note is that you need not assume that your own people cannot do the job of arranging for these services. Look for someone on your staff who has a good head for detail and who does not shy away from new technology. That is just the right person for the job. This becomes more feasible to do in-house if you are not pressed for time. If the time to produce the videoconference is short, hire the outsider, but have one of your people closely involved so that you can eliminate the cost of outside help the next time.

Meeting Management

Most companies have someone on staff who has experience in setting up sales meetings or conventions. If you can get such a person on your project team, you will be in great shape. The reason is that the bulk of the work involved with a videoconference is plain old meeting management. Doing this in-house will save you lots of money because it is this task that accounts for most of the time (and the billing) put in by an outside vendor. Be certain that your meeting manager is up to handling multiple meetings simultaneously. Bring that person into the process immediately so that the scope of the project is clear to him or her. Videoconference meeting management is no different in many respects from management of traditional meetings. There are meals to be scheduled, audiovisual equipment to be ordered, welcome signs to be arranged, sleeping room rosters to be gathered, etc.—but instead of worrying about one meeting at one site, the videoconference will involve the same amount of work at each of many sites, maybe 10, 20, 30 or more. This is complicated by the fact that—unless your time and budget are unlimited—the meeting manager will never be able to do even a site visit to the meeting facilities in the network. One rule of thumb: Assign only about 10 sites to each meeting manager to keep the project controllable. Ideas on making this task more manageable can be found in Chapters 7 and 8.

Talent Coaching

This is one task that, even if you have the world's greatest expert in-house, you should farm out. The reason is that, in most cases, the talent in your videoconference is likely to be of a fairly high executive level. The executive may need a considerable amount of help to perform well in front of a camera, and it is unfair and unrealistic to expect an employee to be honest in critiquing the boss, who has the power to fire or demote. It is much better to have an outsider help executives face the truth about improvements to be made in their presentation technique. Executives will usually accept criticism much more openly from an outsider whom they recognize as an authority than from a subordinate. One overriding factor is that the executives' on-camera competence is *important*. It can make or break your show. And when the show is over, how pleased the executives are with their performance may very well make or break you.

PREPARATION PROBLEMS

Your biggest challenge in the process that begins with planning and extends to air date is keeping your project on time. Planning well can help that, but unforeseen circumstances can throw a clinker into the best-laid plans. Examples? The workbook meant to accompany the program at all locations is delayed at the printer. Your chief scriptwriter comes down with pneumonia. The product that is to be introduced with glorious fanfare fails in test marketing.

To avoid having this type of occurrence cost you money, have a backup plan. Allow yourself plenty of extra fudge-factor time so that you have a cushion you can rely on. Plan a "drop-dead" date to be part of your agreements with all receive site vendors and the production company that describes what will happen. Know in advance what you will have to pay if the entire project is scrubbed.

Act as the overseer who knows at all times how the plan is progressing and who may need help or a reassignment. You never know when you may have to fill the shoes of a key person in the interest of the project.

SUMMARY

Planning is the most important part of any videoconference. Only careful planning gives you the control you need to keep the project moving on time and within everyone's undoubtedly high expectations. Planning will also help you make the most of your in-house personnel, thus saving money. And only with a good backup plan can you handle the unexpected.

5

The Production Process:
Pre-Production Elements

This chapter will help you get the most for your production dollar. Once again, the emphasis will be on planning so that you can remain in control of the project and its costs.

If you are not a professional in this field, it is wise to hire people who have the production skills you need. To get high production quality for a reasonable price, you need to have an understanding of the production business and how a production company operates. This understanding will equip you to deal with production personnel. In dealing with these people it is also necessary to know what questions to ask. The bibliography in the back of this book includes references on television production that may be helpful if you are interested in furthering your knowledge of the subject before beginning your project.

The production process is broken down into three distinct areas:

- pre-production, which involves intensive planning and is generally the most important phase
- production, which involves the recording of material on tape (or film) or shooting live in a studio
- post-production, which involves editing material already recorded on tape (or film)

Post-production will not concern us here because videoconferencing is live. When asked what he liked best about a videoconference project he had just completed, Len Aulenbach of SmithKline said, "It was done when it was done." In other words, there was no post-production.

PRE-PRODUCTION

Pre-production is where the real work is. Pre-production really ought to be spelled p-l-a-n-n-i-n-g because that is the most crucial part. It is during pre-production that all your ideas for your project are laid before professional producers who, in turn, lay before you a plan for accomplishing the task. Then this plan is developed and refined as scripts are written, graphics are produced and sets designed—all within the pre-production cycle. The basic steps involved for a videoconference are (1) selecting a production company, (2) selecting an origination site and (3) developing the production elements.

Selecting a Production Company

Unless you are a producer yourself, you should hire an independent professional to help you shop for a production company, especially for your first project. You will make up the cost of this person over and over in money you will save because he or she will know how to deal with the production companies and keep an eye on them. However, even with a professional in tow, there are some things you should understand about production companies before you start talking to them.

A production company is a business just like any other. The goal of management is to make money. They may not look like typical businesspeople in their jeans, but they have a real interest in selling their product. They will be especially interested in convincing you to use their latest equipment. Why? Because it may still be a novelty to them, they enjoy working with it, and they need to pay it off.

Of course, just as in other businesses, production companies do not survive very long if their customers are not satisfied. So they have a deep interest in producing high-quality programs that they will be proud to use later on in their demo reels. They also want to keep you happy, proudly showing off your new videotape, so that you will come back to them for more of their services and recommend them to your colleagues, as well.

In the interest of increased income production companies will also want to do as much of your project as they possibly can. Sometimes, even if they do not have the necessary experience, they will give it a shot just to keep the business in-house.

Another common characteristic of production companies is that they do not like to give firm bids—in writing. There are some good reasons for that. They are afraid that you will add expensive elements at the last minute and insist that you should not pay extra. Sometimes they don't know how much work a particular project may entail, and they want to cover themselves. However, you are entitled to a firm bid—otherwise, how can you possibly budget your project? To make that bid meaningful, you should be prepared to outline in great detail just what services you will need. That way the production company can feel more comfortable about giving you something in writing, feeling that you know what you're doing.

There are some things that you should think about when you select a production company. Maybe you will end up doing business with a company even though some of these elements are problematic, but at least you will be aware of the risk.

Live TV Experience

The first question you should ask is whether the production company has live television experience. You are likely to find that experience at local television stations because most of them do live news, sports or other events. However, that experience is rare at production houses, which are primarily good at editing videotape.

The "live" qualification is important because the production of live programming is quite different from that of videotape. It requires a crew that is much more alert, experienced and attuned to your project. A videotape production, on the other hand, can be shot, reshot and heavily edited to get the desired effect. In live

TV you have one chance to get the effect you want, and it must be right the first time.

Student Employees

Agree to work only with a completely professional crew. Students are on staff, of course, at most university production centers, but you will also find them working at some public television stations or as interns at other studios. Why is this bad? It can cost you quality, money and time. One example occurred at a television station that employed a great deal of student help. Four students carried props into a studio to be used on a set. Although the props were supposed to be incorporated into the set immediately, the students had too little experience to know how to do this, so after all the carrying was done, they sat down and waited over an hour for a supervisor to come and tell them what to do next. The client paid for that hour for four crew people at the same rate as would have been charged for experienced personnel. This can add to your bill rather quickly as well as subject you to the risk of inexperienced people doing a job improperly.

Providing a Fixed Bid

Simply do not do business with a company that will not give you a fixed bid. Yes, you will need to do your homework to make that bid meaningful, but insist upon it or take your work elsewhere. The advantage for you is that with a fixed bid you will have your budget defined for the project—and no unpleasant surprises to justify to your boss at the end of the project. You will also have some leverage with the company. Clare Mann suggests that for ultimate leverage you get a fixed flat bid for the overall project. Then ask for all the bid's elements to be broken down by hours and price. This will allow you to subtract elements that you don't need or exchange unneeded sevices later on for some eleventh-hour wish.

Plan your needs thoroughly before you go to a production company for a bid. Clare Mann, who has quite a bit of experience in budgeting productions for clients, says that the greatest problem is that people come to him not knowing what they need, or, with a tiny budget. They have no comprehension that you "can't put 10 pounds in a 5 pound sack."

Work Done for Other Clients

See the work of the production company. If it is a local broadcast station, consider what its on-air work looks like. Your production will probably look much the same. Talk to its former clients. Were they pleased? Do they have videotaped samples they can show you? Was the billing from the production company as expected, with no surprises thrown in?

Clare Mann says to "look for high production values, not just a low rate." However, you can expect both high quality and reasonable prices.

Not Operating in a Timely Manner

All projects should progress through a logical series of steps—tasks to be completed at a specified time. Start the production company out with a simple assignment. Give it the final go-ahead only if that assignment is completed on time and in a professional manner. Production is complicated, with later tasks depending upon the completion of earlier ones. You will have a specific air date for your videoconference. You cannot afford for the project to slip.

In summary, here are the main questions you should ask a production company on your first visit:

- Do your people have live television experience?
- Is your crew made up entirely of professionals?
- Will you provide a fixed bid in writing?
- What have you done lately?
- Will you meet deadlines and live up to schedules?

SELECTING THE ORIGINATION SITE

You will have to make a choice regarding the origination point of your videoconference. It need not necessarily originate from a studio, especially if you have some special reason to originate on location. You might have a plant site you want everyone to see or some equipment to demonstrate that is so large that you can't move it into a studio. A location may be indicated because the videoconference is part of something larger—like a convention.

On-location productions can add a wonderful element of excitement to a live program; you give up a little bit of control and gain the advantage of serendipitous occurrences at the site. The down side is that you are at a disadvantage if complete control is critical to you.

Even though a great deal of sophisticated production equipment is available for use outside the studio, you also lose total redundancy (i.e., backups for everything) because carrying two of everything on a location shoot is impractical.

And, of course, location production costs more, since everything that already exists in a controlled studio environment—like lighting or audio—must be set up from scratch when you go on location. That takes time, which translates into money.

Also, in a studio, the crew knows where everything is and how everything works. You can lose a lot of time on location while crew people look for electrical outlets or try to figure out where to park the production van.

Another thing to consider if you decide to originate your production on location is accessibility to a satellite transmitter. (Of course, the same holds true when deciding on a studio, but many of them have ready access to uplinks these days.)

At the very least you will incur extra expense to get your signal from the origination site to the nearest uplink. The best you can hope for is that the site you have chosen is within one microwave "hop" of an uplink. This means that with one shot you can reach an uplink facility using the type of equipment that local news crews use to send live stories to their local stations.

At worst, you will need to rent a transportable uplink— usually a satellite dish mounted on a tractor trailer truck—to come to the location for direct transmission to a satellite. This works well and is recommended. Expect it to add about $5000 to the cost of your project, though.

PLANNING THE PRODUCTION ELEMENTS

During an actual project you will plan your production elements before selecting a production company. However, the production company selection process was discussed first to give you a clearer understanding of why thorough pre-planning is so important.

Before deciding on the exact elements, give some consideration to the approach you'd like to take. Different people, all experienced in the medium, have different opinions on this.

SmithKline's Len Aulenbach, who had had considerable experience in audiovisual presentations before using videoconferencing, says that in the future he "will approach it as a [TV] production, not as a meeting."

Lee Ferguson, in-house producer/director for Procter & Gamble, who has had many years' experience in live commercial television, says, "A videoconference should be entertaining. You get more information across."

Kip Knight, brand manager at Procter & Gamble, likes to be certain his production budget is spent on creativity. "Spend the money you'd otherwise spend on planes in making the meeting distinctive."

Whatever your approach, now is the time to commit it to paper so that the production elements come together and your concept comes alive.

The elements will be covered one at a time. The order of their inclusion does not have any special significance—they're all important.

Pre-Produced Videotape

Although most videoconferences are primarily live television, the majority of them depend upon roll-ins of some pre-produced videotape to add variety. Especially if you choose the safe, but relatively pristine, environment of the studio, a videotape shot on location can add some real sparkle.

Videotaped sequences should be used, though, only when they serve a real purpose in furthering the message of your program. For example, suppose you are describing your all-new production process; show it off on videotape. Make it exciting through skillful editing and the use of a music track.

Some videoconferences are almost entirely videotaped with the only live portion occurring during the question-and-answer session. This is especially useful when dealing with talent that is difficult to work with or when you want the program to move so quickly that nonprofessional talent would just not be able to cope with it. Allow editing to do the coping if you are worried about your talent going live.

Videotaped sequences may be produced especially for your conference, or they may be segments that you already own.

If you do choose to shoot special videotape for your presentation, be sure to allow plenty of time for its production. In that case, a videotape becomes not just a small part of a larger videoconference; it takes on a production life of its own that requires the same careful planning as the videoconference and may take just as much time—especially if a great deal of editing is to be done. One good way to handle this, and not add extra tasks to those involved directly with the videoconference, is to assign the production of the videotape to some entirely different group. Be sure, though, to monitor their progress, because this tape must be ready long before your videoconference air date for review and approval and for technical and dress rehearsals.

Scripts

The script is the guide to the entire production. Only with a good, detailed script will you have a good show. Kip Knight of Procter & Gamble says, "Getting your information from your head to the [audience's] heads is the objective" of any videoconference, and the script is the vehicle that accomplishes this.

It is the script that lays out the complete flow of the program. Some guidelines for scriptwriting come from Clare Mann and Judy Masserang. Mann says that speakers should be on for no longer than six minutes at a time; otherwise, you lose the audience. Masserang believes that the message will hold the audience only if it is either important enough or short enough.

The final script will not only include the words that are to be spoken. It will indicate where the graphics should appear, where the videotape will be rolled in, where your logo should be seen, etc. In short the script is the packaging of the entire program.

An outline of the script will be one of the first things you do to prepare for your videoconference. This script will grow and mature throughout the production process. You will still be working on it at rehearsal time, when the actual words to be spoken will be prepared for use on a teleprompter (see Figure 5.1).

Duration of Program

How long your videoconference lasts depends upon the content itself and the needs of your client. Although it is generally recognized that individual education segments should not last more than 20 minutes or so, some organizations educate their audiences for an hour or more between breaks and are pleased with their results. Of course, you can use a longer segment if your audience is highly motivated to pay attention—as is the case with many professionals, such as attorneys or physicians.

In general, though, for the typical videoconference you should expect to have one 15 minute break for every hour of program. Unless there is some overriding reason for doing so, you should not let the complete program exceed three or four hours. People are just not prepared to sit still for long periods of time. We are all conditioned by commercial television to be able to stand up and leave the room if we want to about every 10 minutes. Forcing people to remain attentive won't work. You will either lose them as they start thinking more about going home than about your content, or they will nod off if there is too much sitting to be done after lunch.

The breaks can serve a dual purpose. Use a short break as a period in which site captains can call in with questions, or use longer ones to hold discussions of the content within local groups.

If you must go with a marathon session, coffee, tea and soft drinks should be available at each receive site throughout the entire program so attendees can take their own minibreaks without having to leave the room.

Figure 5.1: Using a teleprompter during a live videoconference presentation. Photo courtesy SmithKline Beckman.

Set Design

Nothing can add to the cost of a videoconference like a fancy set. Have an idea of the type of set you want before you visit studios, but remain open-minded. Many studios have complete sets in the prop room that may work perfectly well for your presentation. Add your own logo and a plant or two, and you are ready to go at little or no cost.

Most videoconferences will not require an elaborate set. Many can use sets that include the type of consoles seen on news broadcasts or chairs and a couch as on most talk shows. Just be sure that the chairs and couch are not so soft that the talent will sink into them, making it difficult to get up and impossible for female talent to keep their skirts over their knees. Soft chairs and couches also cause people to slouch, which is unattractive on camera.

Some interesting effects can be achieved with a set, so if you have the budget and the creativity to enhance your production through one, do it. One especially effective videoconference set was designed by Procter & Gamble when it introduced Spic and Span Liquid Pine cleaner via satellite. The planner built an entire pine forest of real evergreens inside a studio (see Figure 5.2). The talent sat on stools among the trees throughout most of the presentation.

Live Audience

There are two schools of thought on including a live audience in a studio with the videoconference talent. The jury is still out on whether a studio audience is desirable, but this is one case in which you should let your own opinion carry the day. For the record, here are the schools of thought.

Proponents of the Empty Studio

These people say that television is used most effectively when the speaker is directly addressing the camera lens as if it were a person. By doing that, the speaker appears to be looking directly at the television viewers, as news anchors do. The theory

Figure 5.2: The woods come alive during the satellite introduction of Spic and Span Liquid Pine. Photo courtesy The Procter & Gamble Company.

is that a live audience distracts the speaker's eyes, causing the remote viewers to feel left out of the conversation.

Proponents of Live Audience

Especially for nonprofessional talent, the live audience provides a more natural environment. After all, most people who will appear on a videoconference are probably experienced at speaking in front of live audiences. Len Aulenbach adds that "familiar faces in an audience can help the talent." These proponents do not like the glassy-eyed look that some people get when they must use a teleprompter. An audience gives the speaker another logical and comfortable point with which to make eye contact. Having an audience also gives the camera something else to look at, which can break the monotony of a long presentation. (See Figure 5.3.)

There are other things to consider when deciding on the live

Figure 5.3: A live studio audience provides a more familiar speaking environment that can result in a more relaxed presentation. Photo courtesy SmithKline Beckman.

audience, both pro and con: A live audience can encourage a more spontaneous presentation that does not require a tele-prompter. While this can result in a relaxed, pleasing presentation when done by a professional, more often than not the result is a swaying, moving speaker who is hard to track for the camera people and, thus, distracting to the television audience. Phil Donahue's ability to walk around and appear at ease in front of a camera makes that look simpler than it is.

A real plus for a live audience is that audience members themselves can be called onto the set to participate. This can be particularly effective during a question-and-answer session, when all the company's wisdom cannot possibly fit on one stage.

Graphics and Slides

A variety of graphics can be used to make your production more interesting. Slides, for example, can be used in full screen or in over-the-shoulder shots to show a new product, a chart or statistical information. Be sure that any letters or numbers on the slides are large enough to be easily readable on screen. Check your slides long before air date to give yourself time to make changes or to decide on an alternative. Clare Mann has a sensible tip about slides: "No two slide chains [the mechanism that projects the slide's image] are alike. Plan to go through graphics one by one." Take your completed slides to the studio to be tried on that particular slide chain to be sure that every one of them works.

You may also be creating electronic graphics for use in identifying speakers. Provide a list of all such graphics, with the correctly spelled name and title for each participant. Once these have been prepared by the studio (on a computerized device that allows for easy changes), review them and double-check all spell-ings and titles. Nothing irritates people more than seeing their names misspelled in public. A close second is having the wrong titles attributed to them, especially if the title is lower than their actual rank.

Special Effects

Just about any effect you can imagine—even the spec-tacular effects from the *Star Wars* genre—can be yours in a videoconference. You can add animation. You can make your logo sing and dance. You can flip and fly photographs of your corporate headquarters. You can make your chief executive turn somersaults through space. All this is available at a price. EDS's Judy Masserang finds that most people who come to her are very sophisticated in video and want to use all the latest techniques, but they often find the prices shocking.

Although a special-effect extravaganza can be wildly expensive, most studios can use some effects to spice up your production at a reasonable price. Special effects can be just what you need to grab the attention of your audience. As Kip Knight of Procter & Gamble says, "It's got to be fun. You're competing with TV, music and music videos. Put Hollywood into it."

Another type of effect that may not be considered particularly special can add considerable punch for minimal extra cost. That's stereo. Procter & Gamble has used it to great effect in videoconferencing, and Clare Mann, who has worked with P&G on those projects, says that with stereo the remote audiences are more likely to feel the energy that is going on in the studio.

Stereo is fairly easy to add. You will need two audio channels in the studio. Keep the channels separate through the uplink and use two separate audio subchannels (no extra cost) on your satellite transponder. There are other, more sophisticated ways to go stereo, but this one is easy and virtually free.

PLANNING THE QUESTION-AND-ANSWER EQUIPMENT

How you handle your question-and-answer session (Q&A) will be important to the production studio and can affect the price of your production.

The first thing that can increase the cost is incoming phone lines. If you think your videoconference is going to generate a large number of questions, you may want to consider having one incoming line for each site. However, this is not usually necessary. As long as your site captains are alerted to the fact that they may receive a busy signal during the Q&A, and as long as your phone operators are well coached in keeping calls short, you can do just as well with one incoming line for every two or three sites.

If you do not expect a barrage of calls, you can manage with even fewer lines.

Check with the studio from which your program will be originating. It may already have incoming lines that you can use. This is especially true at public television stations, which generally have several lines available due to their periodic fund-raising campaigns. If you don't need to order phone lines, you can save hundreds or thousands of dollars.

A way to save money if you are originating the program at your own office location is to use the incoming phone lines that your company already owns. Many companies have sophisticated internal systems that make it easy to add lines or special phone numbers. A real advantage in using an internal system is that your own staff people can do the phone work for you, and you will not need to get tangled in the process of ordering special services from your local phone company.

Here are some notes from Clare Mann about ordering phones:

- If you must order equipment or lines from the phone company or some other vendor, order them 30 days in advance and have them installed 5 days in advance because you will need the extra days to get problems corrected through the bureaucracies of most phone companies.
- Be very clear on what you need. Will you need a hunt system, in which the next phone rings if one instrument is in use? Know the number of separate lines you will need and whether you will require an 800 number.
- Beware of inexperienced vendors. Use only a phone company you can really trust. An independent entrepreneur who does not know the facility can be just one more headache.

Mann tells a story that illustrates the kinds of difficult situations you can get into with a phone vendor who is trying to install equipment on unfamiliar ground. He says that for one conference the phone vendor started installing extra lines and instruments a week before air date. Because he did not know

Pre-Production Elements 63

Table 5.1: Budget for a Typical In-Studio Live Videoconference (Three Full Eight-Hour Days of Production)

Studio (including audio equipment and switcher)......	$2,400
3 cameras, with operators	1,260
2 videotape machines.............................	1,500
Film chain	240
Simple special effects............................	300
Character generator	120
Lighting and technician...........................	900
Stage crew (not including set building)..............	800
Director/producer................................	2,000
Production assistant	400
Technical director................................	600
Audio person	400
Videotape person................................	300
Teleprompter and operator........................	380
Floor director	400
10 incoming phone lines and instruments............	3,000
	$15,000 + or − 20%

where all the hookups were in the building, and because he kept discovering additional equipment he needed but had not brought with him, the installation was still going on an hour before air time. Even after Q&A operators had arrived and settled around a large conference table to begin their work, the vendor was still crawling around on the floor at their feet hooking up connectors and looking for loose wires. Eventually the phones were ready to go. But it was the type of situation that did not need to occur at a time when everyone had other things to think about.

SAMPLE BUDGET

Now that you have planned your elements, you are ready to ask your production companies for firm competitive bids.

The budget outlined in Table 5.1 is roughly what you should expect to see for an in-studio production that involves three days of studio time:

- one day to set, block and hold a technical rehearsal
- one day to rehearse with talent
- one day to go on air

The prices listed in the budget are average, plus or minus about 20%. The higher prices will be found in New York or Los Angeles, but regardless of where you are, if your videoconference is fairly simple and the prices are much higher than this, you should ask questions and get other bids, because something is wrong.

In general a studio will give you a package price rather than break down the components. In our budget, prices of individual services are included to give you an idea of the relative value of the pieces to use as a guide in adding, deleting or using service prices in bargaining. The prices themselves, and the packaging of the components, will vary greatly. However, the information is provided here as an encouragement to negotiate by deleting from a studio's package services that you do not really need. This price list also shows clearly that adding extra services can increase your costs, especially if you add those extra services at the last minute and incur overtime charges.

(Some of the differences in estimates for people are due to both the relative value of personnel—e.g., a producer obviously costs more than a teleprompter operator—and the fact that some personnel will spend more time on the project than others.)

SUMMARY

Pre-production involves planning to the nth degree. A television production, especially a live one, is a complex process that requires that all elements be carefully laid out. It is during the pre-production phase that these details are translated into bids, preferably firm and in writing, from production companies with experience in live television. This phase will make it possible for the rehearsal and on-air production to flow smoothly, resulting in a show of which you can be proud.

6

The Production Process: From Rehearsal to On-Air

Now that the research is done, your plan is on paper, and the production company and studio have been hired, you are ready to pull everything together to go on air.

Your script will probably include all the basic videoconference elements: a network sign-on, network countdown, program open, main presentation, break, Q&A and close. You are now ready to integrate these elements into a cohesive program.

At this point you will be working closely with the production company and studio personnel to take advantage of their specialized capabilities.

TIMING

Since this is live television, your timing will have to be impeccable. Use your detailed script to time the production to the minute. Go over the timing in technical and dress rehearsals to find portions of the script that may need to be cut or added to. In the unfamiliar environment of a studio, reading from a teleprompter, your talent may find themselves progressing more slowly or more quickly than expected.

You will have bought only a certain amount of satellite time. To take advantage of it you will want to start on time—to the second. Also, when your time is up, it's up. There may be someone right behind you waiting to use that same transponder. If you find, though, that you would like the security of being able to run your program a little longer than planned (perhaps you will decide to extend the Q&A if the response is good) simply buy an extra half hour or so of satellite time as an insurance policy.

SYSTEM TEST PRODUCTION

Another element tied to the timing of your production is the system test. Plan to have at least an hour of system test to allow your receive sites time to tune in to your transponder and take care of technical adjustments. It is important to decide well in advance what the makeup of this test will be so that the downlink technicians will know what to look for. A typical system test might be the following:

- 10 minutes of color bars and tone
- 10 minutes of videotape with music
- graphics incorporated over these elements asking site captains to call the origination site and check in
- graphics prepared to address specific sites that have not checked in as requested
- continuation throughout the test of videotape and music with superimposed graphics that count down the minutes until the beginning of the show

These elements, as simple as they are, should be produced and ready a couple of days before air date. That will be just one less element to worry about at broadcast time.

INJECTING SPONTANEITY

The beauty of live television is that it can be spontaneous. Lee Ferguson, now with Procter & Gamble, who has spent much of his production career working in live commercial television, is a supporter of the value of spontaneity. He says, "Some moments may be heartwarming or silly. But you can't script these, and they make the show special. The personality comes through." Of course, rehearsals that give the talent a chance to become familiar with the process help ease the way to spontaneity, and sometimes it is necessary to build in opportunities for it. Otherwise, especially on a first production, nonprofessional talent can simply look too stiff.

Both Procter & Gamble and SmithKline Beckman have used spontaneity to great advantage in their videoconferences. In its introduction of Spic and Span Liquid Pine cleaner, Procter & Gamble arranged for an employee dressed in a bear suit to appear in the pine woods built for the occasion and creep up behind the unsuspecting Q&A panel members, growling menacingly. The bear helped enliven an otherwise dry, fact-filled Q&A and was mentioned favorably by many of the remote audience members who responsed to an evaluation afterward.

SmithKline used a studio audience for spontaneity. When one of the panel members—once again during Q&A—did not have a good answer to an incoming question, he invited a knowledgeable audience member to come on stage and take over. The audience member had no idea that such a thing might happen, and there was a lot of good-natured joking as he figured out how to use the microphone, which was firmly attached to the tie of the panel member. That joking loosened up the entire panel, and the remainder of the Q&A was much more effective than the earlier portion, which had featured the executive talent lined up in a row on stage, looking concerned about whether they would answer the questions correctly (see Figure 6.1).

Q & A

That Q&A portion, by the way, can actually be the most important part of your videoconference, and you should plan on giving it the time and attention it deserves.

After all, the point of most videoconferences is to impart information to a remote audience. That information is shared through videotapes, live speeches, graphics, demonstrations and more. But what really makes a videoconference pay for itself is the opportunity for interactivity that it allows. And that is the Q&A portion. That is when the audience talks back to the presenters and shares its own points of view while asking questions.

There are three ways to handle Q&A:

Figure 6.1: A panel of construction industry experts on the set of an Associated Builders and Contractors videoconference. Photo courtesy Associated Builders and Contractors, Inc.

1. Unscreened, live, foldback audio. This live method makes many people nervous. The actual voice of the questioner is heard in the studio and simultaneously over the television systems at all remote sites. This can add spontaneity with a capital *S* and has been used to great effect by Chrysler. However, Gerry Hendrixson of Procter & Gamble considers this type of Q&A too risky because the talent has "no time to think about the questions" before giving an answer. Sometimes the answers are too critical to be given off the cuff.

2. Live, foldback audio with screening. This looks the same as the method above but adds an element of safety. In this method the caller is not placed on the air immediately. Instead the call comes to a phone operator. The operator ascertains the nature of the question—to be sure it is pertinent, that it has not already been asked,

and that the caller seems unlikely to say anything un-
seemly on live television. The caller is put on hold, is
asked by an audio operator to repeat the question, and
then the talent is notified through cue cards or an earpiece that a caller is waiting. (see Figure 6.2.) The caller
then goes on air. This method was used with good effect
in a televised seminar on long-distance running, which
featured several well-known personalities on the panel. It
allowed the moderator the control to take calls when he
felt the timing was right. He always knew that a call was
ready—and from what city—through an earpiece.

3. Screened, written questions. This is the method favored
by most corporations since it offers the ultimate in control. In this case there is a break in the program while the
audience is invited to call with its questions. Phone oper-

Figure 6.2: Screening questions in the phone room of a videoconference origination site. Photo courtesy Associated Builders and Contractors, Inc.

Figure 6.3: Panel members responding to questions that have been screened, then written on 4 × 6 cards. Photo courtesy The Procter & Gamble Company.

ators write down the questions on 4 x 6 cards. These are then screened by company employees for pertinence and redundancy. The questions are generally sorted by topic. Sometimes the answers are written on the card as an aid to the on-air talent. The cards are then given to the talent, who are ready to answer questions when the program comes back on air. These questions can continue to be delivered throughout the live Q&A until the session is over (see Figure 6.3). Often the written questions that are not answered due to time constraints are answered later over the phone or through the mail.

Plan well in advance who will be involved in this Q&A portion. You will need phone operators (company employees are the best since they'll understand the jargon that is likely to be part of the questions), screeners and runners to take the questions to the talent.

Prepare a graphic of the phone number to keep on air to encourage more questions to come in even while others are being answered.

MAKEUP/CLOTHING

Several days before going on air alert your talent to the fact that they should give some serious consideration to what they will wear on camera and that they must expect to have makeup applied. A little makeup can go a long way to eliminate dark circles under the eyes, and the proper suit or dress can create a look of competence and confidence for the speaker. (see Figure 6.4.) Here are some general guidelines to follow. Copy them to give to your talent before rehearsal day.

Men

Clothing

Men should follow these rules:

- Wear comfortable clothing. Don't wear a new shirt or suit for the first time.
- Wear a dark, solid-color suit and a blue or other pastel shirt.
- Avoid ties with complicated stripes or other patterns that may cause a strobing effect on camera.
- Wear long, dark socks.
- Wear cool clothing. If you tend to perspire heavily even in winter, wear a lightweight suit.

Makeup

Here are some suggestions for makeup:

- Makeup may not be needed. However, bald men should bring some powder to help avoid the shine caused by overhead lights.

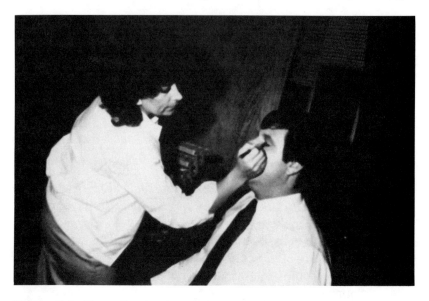

Figure 6.4: Executive having makeup applied before going on air. A professional makeup artist is used to assure that the talent makes the best possible television appearance. Photo courtesy The Procter & Gamble Company.

- If needed, it should be applied by a professional with the primary goal of eliminating dark shadows under the eyes and to make the eyes appear larger.

Hair

- Bring a comb and ask to see yourself on a monitor before air time.
- Comb away any obvious stray strands.

Women

Clothing

Women should follow these guidelines:

- Wear dark colors.
- Avoid white and light pastels close to the face.

- Avoid dangling jewelry that will catch the studio lights and be distracting on camera.
- Wear comfortable clothing. Don't wear a new dress or suit for the first time.
- Avoid wearing a skirt that will need tugging to be kept over your knees.
- Avoid patterns or stripes that may cause strobing on camera.

Makeup

Here are suggestions for makeup:

- Use a little extra powder to avoid a shiny nose.
- Lipstick with a bluish tint tends to make the teeth look whiter.
- Add makeup to accentuate the eyes slightly more heavily than for street wear.

Hair

- Avoid hairdos that include bangs close to the eyes.
- Bring a comb and use the studio monitor to check your appearance.

General

Remember, the camera will see what you want it to see. Your TV appearance will make a lasting impression with many people. Take special care to look and feel your best for any TV appearance.

SCHEDULING

By this point your production schedule should be ironclad. Be certain to notify your talent as far in advance as possible— weeks if you can—as to the date, time and place of rehearsals. Your talent will probably be executives with busy schedules,

who will appreciate the notice. Last-minute scheduling of rehearsals that results in the absence of any presenter can mean
real disaster at air time. Here is an idea of what your schedule
should look like:

- three days before air time: set, light, technical rehearsal
- two days before air time: nothing, you hope. (This is a
  buffer in case any polishing needs to be done to follow up
  the previous day's work.)
- one day before air time: talent rehearsal
- air date

Many times this schedule is expanded to allow for more
talent rehearsals, often using a company-owned videotape camera. Procter & Gamble also makes sure to schedule its dress
rehearsal at least a week before air date. The crew tapes that
rehearsal and sends a copy to each meeting site—where tape
players have been installed with the monitors—to use in case
absolute disaster at one or more meeting sites makes it impossible for the live videoconference to be received. The staff then
plans a minirehearsal for early on the morning of the air date.

Technical Rehearsal

Technical rehearsal gives the production crew an opportunity to walk through the complete show to work out any bugs.
Crew members are used to play the parts of the talent. This
serves two purposes: (1) it does not waste the executives' time,
since a considerable amount of standing around is inevitable
while lights are adjusted, different cameras angles are tested,
etc.; and (2) it gives the crew a chance to understand the program
and its purposes by playing the parts of the executives.

Clare Mann says that, sad but true, in most cases each
videoconference is just one more job assignment for the crew.
The crew members do not care about the individual client, only
about doing their jobs. A crew can become competent only with
rehearsal. Mann says, "Take the crew and involve them in the
situation." And, if your camera crew seems shaky, write down
every shot as a guide and never hesitate to get rid of a bad camera
person. That person's role is too important.

Procter & Gamble's Lee Ferguson also stresses the value of this technical rehearsal. "Get to know the crew. Get to know their strengths and weaknesses." This is extremely important in most videoconference situations, in which a corporate producer may be involved only on rare occasions with a given television crew. Bear in mind the cold fact that if an incompetent or poorly rehearsed crew causes your production to look bad, you will look bad. The most wonderful scripts, graphics and planning are wasted if your crew does not help you bring them together into a cohesive package.

Talent Rehearsal

Once again, keep in mind that your performers are probably very busy executives. Use their time wisely. Let them know what time to arrive for makeup (yes, use makeup for rehearsal) and what time the actual rehearsal will start. Plan for the rehearsal to take about twice as long as the actual program. You should have already worked out major bugs at the technical rehearsal. *Stick to these schedules.* Doing so will enhance your own reputation for competence.

To prevent the loss of time as crew members leave the premises to eat and straggle back from various restaurants, holding up the entire process, you should plan to have a caterer bring in lunch for the entire cast and crew.

There is nothing magical about rehearsal. It is simply practice, practice that can make your show a real success. Rehearsal offers insurance that your live program will be as good as possible. Some comments on the importance of rehearsal from the pros:

- Clare Mann: "A bad show makes the talent look bad. You lose credibility. You leave a bad taste in a lot of people's mouths."
- "Rehearsal is by far the most important element. Too many people say let's do [the entire program] in one day. It just doesn't work. You put yourself in a position where you make errors and the show looks bad."
- Judy Masserang: "[A show] that's done badly will be long remembered."

Rehearsal makes a good show likely. Absence of rehearsal makes disaster likely. Never agree to do a live television production without adequate rehearsal.

Rehearsal is also when the help of the outside producer is especially valuable. Clare Mann says that the producer who is not directly on the client company's payroll "can approach a corporate executive with criticism, calm him down and make him feel like a real person without fear of firing."

Lee Ferguson sees the role of producer in much the same light. He says, "Get to know the participants. Break down the barriers between president and producer."

An important thing to make known to executive talent is that the producer, whether an outsider or an insider, is there to make the talent look good. Only if the talent looks good will the program be a success. And the program's success will be the measure of the producer's own performance.

Before rehearsal starts be certain that all scripts are prepared for teleprompter and proofread. Be certain that everything is in place just as it will be for the actual program. There should be no planned difference between the rehearsal and the live program. It is critical that the rehearsal leaves the talent and crew confident of their ability to do a good job and confident that no surprises await them while they are on the air live.

Taping the Event

On the day of your event tape the entire production. Perhaps you will use this only for archival purposes. But the tape may have some additional value. More about that in Chapter 11.

MANAGING THE DAY OF THE EVENT

With any live production, the day of the event should bring a feeling of theatrical excitement to the proceedings. That may cause jitters, but it should also prompt a rush of energy that will enhance the overall program.

At this point, all hands should be well rehearsed and familiar with their roles. You should need to worry only about logistics.

- Arrive early. Ask the crew to arrive early—at least four hours before you are due to go on air. This will give you a little fudge time in case there are any last-minute details to clear up.
- To make early arrival a little more palatable, provide coffee and rolls for the crew.
- Plan to have a catered lunch for crew and talent, to avoid losing them to traffic or crowded restaurants at a critical moment.
- Go over all graphics one more time. In particular, check for spellings of names.
- Assign an assistant to help run errands for you if things start to get a little crazy. Even if things are not crazy, your nerves will make you think they are.
- Have your talent arrive about an hour before air time for makeup.
- If there is to be a studio audience, seat them about 15 minutes before you go on air.
- Double-check all microphones.
- If you are using wireless microphones, be sure that only new, fresh batteries are being used.
- Place water and glasses on stage in accessible places for the talent.
- Start your system test exactly on time to avoid confusing your remote sites.
- You're on the air.

SUMMARY

The production portion of your program is the culmination of weeks, maybe months, of detailed planning. This is the part where your program concept coalesces and comes alive as you actually go on air. It is extremely important—and the only way to assure a quality program—to insist upon complete and well-planned rehearsals. As Clare Mann notes, "People are complex and don't always operate at the same speed." Rehearsal helps synchronize the people with the production elements.

7

Networking

The correct, efficient and effective execution of a network is the single most difficult task in videoconferencing. It is difficult because the efforts of so many technicians in cities around the United States or the world must be coordinated into one cohesive, climactic, simultaneous event that must appear flawless. This chapter will explain how to make all the pieces come together in an orderly way. A checklist will be included at the end to recap the steps that must be taken to ensure success.

First, an explanation of what we mean by networking: For our purposes, networking is simply bringing together into a workable entity all of the services, equipment and people involved in a videoconference project from the first transmission of a signal at the origination point, through the satellite, to the receive equipment at many locations and back again,—i.e., all the way from the sending of the signal until it reaches the eyes and ears of the audience and their responses have come back.

In a network involving 20 cities, 60 or more vendors may play a part. Each will have a separate, and often unique, task to perform. Each should be a trained professional who understands how his or her task is related to all the others.

There are five major elements in a videoconference network:

- the satellite
- the uplink and related transmission
- the downlinks
- audiovisual equipment
- meeting rooms

CHOOSING A SATELLITE

Two main considerations and some minor ones must be kept in mind when deciding which satellite to use.

One crucial consideration is the satellite's "footprint," that section of the earth's surface that is capable of receiving its signal (see Chapter 1).

The choice of a satellite with a correct footprint becomes important once you have your network of receive cities determined. For example, if you will have receive locations spread across the United States from Maine to California, a satellite centrally located above the center of North America with a full continental U.S. (CONUS) footprint will be just the right choice. If your network consists of just the Western states plus Hawaii, a single satellite positioned over the Western portion of North America will work. If you add Europe to your domestic network, no single satellite will do the job. You'll need at least two to reach the entire area, plus an extra uplink to act as a relay to retransmit the signal from the first to the second satellite.

You need not be a technical expert, though, to deal with this. You will probably be ordering your satellite time from a company (such as Wold or Bonneville) that owns large blocks of time on many different satellites or from a broker (such as Sat Time) that has access to it on satellites owned by many different companies. The personnel of these companies are generally quite knowledgeable and can be a great help to you in deciding which satellite to use. When you call, be prepared to describe your network and give the date and time of day you will need the service and the duration of your program. They will match your requirements with what they have available. However, if you think you may not be getting what you need, you should call another company and shop around. At this writing there is more satellite time than there are buyers, so the chances of getting what you want are high.

The second critical consideration in selecting a satellite involves the technical mode of transmission—most typically C-band (4 to 6 GHz) or Ku-band (12 to 14 GHz). Which one you choose depends upon your needs. First, C-band is less expensive (about $300 per hour compared with $600 an hour for Ku-band), but in the grand scheme of a videoconference, the price of satellite time is so minimal that its cost rarely plays a significant part in making a choice. Other differences mean much more.

C-band

At this writing C-band is used for transmission by PBS, CBS, ABC, HBO, ESPN and every other cable service. That means that, unless you scramble your signal (more about that later in this chapter) a high percentage of America will be able to pick up your signal freely. Most backyard satellite dishes are C-band so that their owners can pick up a wide variety of cable signals, and your signal will be traveling right along with them.

Another disadvantage of C-band is that it is highly suscepti-ble to interference from other microwave sources (satellite sig-nals themselves operate on microwaves). One of the biggest problems here is that telephone companies also use C-band to send and receive phone signals. Most cities are virtually blanketed by these invisible phone company signals, which wreak havoc with C-band video transmission, making it abso-lutely impossible to receive C-band signals at many sites; metro-politan areas suffer the worst.

A redeeming feature of C-band is that it has been around the longest and therefore most of the receive dishes around are C-band. For that reason, if easy, accessible blanket coverage is your goal—and you have no concern for security—you should go with C-band.

Ku-band

Ku-band is used for transmission by NBC and several cor-porations in their private networks, and that's about it. Since so few are tuned to it, Ku is certainly more secure. You can be relatively certain that backyard users are not receiving it.

Especially in its early days, Ku-band was rumored to be unduly susceptible to severe rain attenuation, which resulted in degraded or total loss of signal in heavy rain or snow conditions. NBC disproved this rumor with extensive testing before deciding to deliver the complete network via Ku. Does rain attenuation exist? Yes, so the technicians say, but mainly on their scopes. To the layman, the worst that a rain- or snowstorm brings to Ku-band is a little sparkle on the screen.

The big advantage to Ku-band, though, is that it operates on a different frequency from that of your local phone company. Thus, it is much less likely to experience signal interference. If you can see the sky in the direction of your desired satellite, even in a metropolitan area, you can probably receive a Ku-band signal. This is why Ku-band has become so popular in fixed corporate networks for companies with downtown locations. (see Figure 7.1.)

One minor consideration in choosing a satellite is frequency of use. This can affect cost. If you choose the most popular piece of satellite real estate—e.g., the "birds" that carry HBO, ESPN, and their counterparts—you will pay a hefty price, probably a couple of thousand dollars an hour.

Another, more mundane, concern relates to the site survey and the testing aspects. Unless the downlinker you hire has used the same satellite at your chosen location on another occasion, there will have to be a site survey. In many cases a technician will actually arrive with a downlink dish to assess the quality of signal that can be picked up at the site from the satellite you have chosen. Before your system test, on the day of your event, the technician will also focus the downlink by tuning into whatever is being broadcast on that particular transponder.

If you choose a satellite that is infrequently used—maybe one that has just been launched—your downlinkers will not be able to tune in to your transponder for their surveys or tests. Therefore, until you go on air with your own test signal you will not know for sure how efficient that satellite is at that location. It is best to rent an often-used satellite to avoid adding one more worry to your network. Let someone else be the pioneer on a new satellite.

UPLINKING

Now that your satellite has been chosen, you are ready to shop for your uplink. An uplink is a dish that transmits a signal to a satellite. If you plan to receive a Ku signal, the uplink must

Figure 7.1: A transportable Ku-band uplink preparing to transmit from a downtown Cincinnati location. Photo courtesy The Procter & Gamble Company.

operate in Ku (you can turn around one variety of signal to access downlinks of another by taking it down at a location that has the desired type of uplink and retransmitting it.) If you plan to receive in C-band, your uplink must operate in C-band. There are many reliable uplinkers available. Virginia Ostendorf's *Uplink Directory* (see Bibliography) can be a real help in finding an uplinker. In many cases, though, the studio you have selected for your transmission will already have an established relationship with an uplink company, and you will not need to worry too much about this. For uplinking services, expect to pay from $125 to $300 per hour.

If there is no uplink at your origination site, you can still have uplink access. There are two ways:

1. A ground connection of some variety. This may be a microwave system of the type used by local news crews, or it may be a telephone company landline connection. Expect to pay about $250 to $500 an hour for the microwave connection. Phone company landline charges range from hundreds to thousands of dollars, although some studios have permanent phone company connections that are reasonably priced. Be careful when ordering phone company landlines. Ordering must take place very early. Moreover, in some smaller towns, telephone company crews are not familiar with video landlines (different from voice grade lines), and much confusion can result.
2. A transportable uplink. Although transportable uplinks are getting smaller, you can still expect your transportable uplink to arrive on a tractor trailer rig (see Figure 7.2). A day's use of a transportable uplink will range in cost from $4500 to $7500, depending upon the company that delivers it and where it happens to be before it drives to your location. You pay the mileage. The transportable uplinking business, though, is highly competitive, so it pays to shop.

If you decide to use the transportable uplink, plan to have a complete survey of your origination site early in the planning stage. You must be sure you can park the tractor trailer rig off the

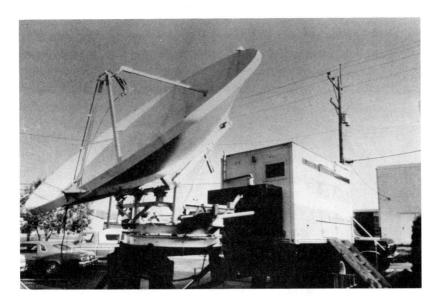

Figure 7.2: A transportable uplink dish being used at a suburban television studio that has no uplink of its own. Photo courtesy The Procter & Gamble Company.

city streets, near enough to reach the control room by cable and still within view of the portion of the sky where your satellite is orbiting. Plan to have both the uplink and its engineer arrive the day before your transmission. This may cost you extra, but it will be worth it. It will give you time to check out and correct any problems that may have resulted from transporting the uplink or any problems related to accessing the control room. (see Figure 7.3.) One more tip: Since the transportable unit will probably be parked in an exposed location, plan to hire a security guard to keep an eye out for vandals during the hours when production personnel will not be present.

DOWNLINKS

There are two general types of downlinks available to the user (besides Ku- or C-band). These are (1) "fixed" or (2) transportable downlinks. A fixed downlink is one that permanently resides at a location. It is either bolted into concrete or attached to the roof (see Figure 7.4). It also has permanent cable connections into meeting rooms.

This permanency is a real plus. It generally means that the system has been used frequently and is thoroughly debugged. However, don't let anybody talk you into skipping a thorough

Figure 7.3: Engineer inside a transportable uplink truck checking the controls before beginning transmission. Photo courtesy The Procter & Gamble Company.

Figure 7.4: This roof-mounted fixed downlink, located at Howard University Law School in Washington, DC, is part of the American Law Network. Photo courtesy COMSAT General Corp.

system test just because the network seems stable. Anything could have gone wrong since the last transmission—e.g., a blown fuse, a cut cable—and you do not want to find out about it at air time. Fixed downlinks can be found at some hotel chains (Holiday Inns have more than anyone else), colleges and some corporate locations. The cost of a fixed downlink is difficult to break out, because most facilities that have them build the price into the meeting room charges.

A transportable downlink is one that is wheeled from site to site as needed on a small trailer attached to the back of a car or truck. These actually tend to be quite reliable. Perhaps expecting the possibility of problems, the technicians are more sensitive to keeping them in good condition and to the need for thorough testing. The wonderful thing about transportable downlinks is that any location with electricity and a view of the proper part of the sky can become a receive site. This means that your office, your manufacturing plants or your boss's home can be part of your videoconference network. And you can use a combination of fixed downlinks and transportables. Expect to pay from $750 to $1000 per day for a transportable downlink. Virginia Ostendorf's *Downlink Directory* (see Bibliography) can be a big help in finding both fixed and transportable downlinks.

DEALING WITH TECHNICIANS

Most downlink technicians are professionals. They know their business and can even be a good source of information in scouting out likely receive sites in a strange city.

Just as in dealing with most service people, it pays to get to know your downlinker, even if it is over the phone. Let the technician know what you are trying to accomplish and what your concerns are. Judy Masserang of EDS says that she tries to develop rapport with downlinkers so that they feel as if they are doing the job for a friend.

You should also try not to be shy about asking for a discount when you are dealing directly with the downlink vendor. In most networks, the downlink vendor is not dealing directly with the end user, but with a middleman—e.g., a professional networking company such as VideoStar or Satellease. The professional networker charges the end user $1000 or more per downlink, pays the individual downlink vendor about $750 and pockets the rest as profit. You can get your downlink at the same price as the professional networker if you know enough to ask. If you don't, you may find yourself being billed $1000 per downlink, with the additional $250 going into the downlinker's pocket.

Plan on getting price guarantees for your downlink up front. Included in the appendix is a form that we have used in two parts to guarantee prices. Once the prices were discussed over the phone, we filled out the form outlining the services and prices that had been agreed upon. Then the form was mailed to the downlinker for signature and return of one copy. This caused us a little paperwork, but it also resolved one or two price disputes for us quite easily.

SETTING UP THE DOWNLINKS

Four hours before a videoconference is about to begin is generally enough time for the transportable vendor to be at the receive site, less for the fixed downlink technician. Plan to start your system test about two hours before actual transmission to give the downlinker plenty of time to tune and tweak the equipment.

If you plan to start your transmission in the early morning, Eastern Time, you may want your West Coast downlinkers and audiovisual technicians to set up the night before. This will make their lives a little easier and will save you some anxiety on the morning of the event. In all cases in which the technicians must be on the job in the early hours, make sure you have their beeper or home phone numbers in case they fail to arrive on time and you have to track them down.

Usually, the following schedule works quite well:

1. Four hours before transmission time the downlinker arrives on site. The technician calls a central point to check in and confirm that he or she has arrived.
2. Between arrival time and system test time, the downlinker will be setting up. You should be kept informed by the downlinker if any problems arise. You or an engineer

at the origination site may be able to help solve a problem. In the worst case, you need to know when it's necessary to call a backup technician.

3. Two hours before program time, a transmission of a system test begins. Your downlink technician should have received from you well in advance complete instructions that include:

   a. identification of satellite, transponder and audio subchannels to be used

   b. where to call to check in during system test

   c. backup phone number in case something is wrong with the system test number

   d. the name of the person in charge at the origination site

   e. an agenda of the day's programming events, including expected time of breaks (the technician may need the break to make an equipment adjustment)

   f. what will be included in the system test

   g. the name of the local site captain who is acting as host for the end user

   h. the name of the meeting site employee with whom you have been dealing

   i. the name and phone number of the audiovisual company and of the technician who is working at the site

If you provide a full set of instructions and information to the downlinker, that technician can be your best friend and a good representative for you. The technician, armed with complete information, will feel in control of the situation and will be prepared to help out with other problems at the receive site should they occur.

Our projects have been saved many times by technicians who knew what the objective at the site was and went the extra mile to make something work or to talk the meeting site personnel into some desirable last-minute service. The thing that really comes to mind here is telephones in the meeting rooms for the Q&A session. Somehow, regardless of how often a hotel promises a phone in the room—even in writing—the staff always seems surprised on the day of the event that you actually need the instrument. Downlinkers can be very helpful in tracking down missing phones.

AUDIOVISUAL EQUIPMENT

It is not always necessary to engage additional technicians to set up and run your audiovisual equipment. Often these days, downlink suppliers are stocking and becoming proficient at a/v and vice versa. The combination can be quite good. It gives you the capability to negotiate for a package price that can be lower than it would be if you were buying downlinking and a/v separately.

The most expensive way to order a/v equipment is directly through a hotel, where there is a hefty markup placed on it. Usually, the way it works is this. A local a/v dealer has a permanent office in the hotel. Such dealers provide the equipment from their own warehouses but, since it is billed through the hotel, a 15% to 20% markup is added. Sometimes you think you are taking less of a risk by ordering through the hotel because the equipment is already on site and will not have to be transported for your event. Indeed, hotel a/v offices often claim that this is the case. In fact, however, experience shows that the type of equipment needed for videoconferences is rarely in stock at hotels, so you run the risk of transport and still pay the higher price.

Call a/v dealers directly. Even if you happen upon the dealer who has the hotel office, you may still benefit from the 15% to 20% lower price by dealing directly. Ask for that discount and expect to get it. If you don't, shop elsewhere. We have not found a hotel yet that will exclude the a/v dealer of your choice from its property. A good source for a/v is the *NAVA/ICIA Membership Directory* (see Bibliography).

Get your prices and services guaranteed—in writing—just as you did with the downlinkers. In fact, the same form (found in the Appendix) can be used. You should also provide your a/v technician with the same detailed information you have given the downlinkers.

Here's what you'll need.

Projection Equipment

Unless you plan to have fewer than six people in a very small room, plan on a large-screen video system. About six feet in diagonal is large enough for groups up to about 100. As the group grows, you can go to nine feet or larger. In some cases the size of the projection equipment is not entirely dependent upon audience size. Other factors such as room configuration or ceiling height can determine just how large you can go. Rely on your a/v dealer at the site to advise you. If the a/v technician is not familiar with the property, ask him or her to visit the site and scout out the room. You will generally not be charged extra for this service. Doing this survey is of benefit to the a/v dealer, too, because it will alert him or her to potential problems and to the optimum equipment for the site.

Always plan to have a backup projection system. Some groups are content to use two or more smaller monitors (19 inches or 25 inches) as backup to the large-screen projection system. Sometimes these small monitors are set up and played at the sides of the large-screen system throughout the event. These multiple screens of differing sizes are very distracting to the audience. If you plan to use them, hook them up, but leave them turned off unless needed.

In most cases, it is best to have a backup projection unit identical to the main unit. With most equipment this means an extra projector only, not an extra screen. The switch can be made quickly in case of trouble. An identical backup unit will not cost much more than two small monitors and will be a whole lot more pleasing to the audience if it really needs to be used.

Prices vary for large-screen systems throughout the country, but you can expect them to range from $500 to $750 for the main unit and an identical backup projector for half that. Prices can run as high as $1000 for the main unit in New York or Los Angeles, but these are exceptions.

As we noted in our discussion of downlinker's pricing, these price ranges are those that you should expect to pay if you order directly from an a/v supplier. Should you engage a professional networker to order a/v for you, expect to pay $1000 to $1500 per site, with the networker pocketing the difference.

You may also need supplemental audio. In newer hotels, the incoming audio signal usually sounds just fine over the available P.A. system, but in older hotels—or if your videoconference features music—plan on ordering additional audio equipment. Once again, have the a/v dealer survey the meeting site and advise you on what you need. These people are amazingly honest about suggesting when more equipment is needed—they are professionals who want your repeat business. Besides, a complete audio system does not cost very much—about $150 or so a day—and can enhance a program.

A/V Setup

Plan to have your audiovisual technicians and equipment arrive about four hours before show time, along with the downlink. This allows everything to be set up concurrently for easy interfacing of all the equipment.

If your program is to begin early in the Eastern Time zone, you will want to have the a/v equipment delivered the night before on the West Coast. Most meeting sites have no objection to using the meeting room the night before for storage and will probably not charge you a fee to do so. To avoid a fee, though, be prepared to make your delivery late at night, after the previous user of the room is gone.

Both in setting up the night before or in setting up early in the morning, it is likely that the room with its equipment will be unattended for some period of time. Instruct your a/v dealer to have the security guard at the meeting site lock the doors once the delivery has been made. Instances of theft of equipment or tampering with controls are isolated, but you won't want to be surprised with either of them on the day of the broadcast.

Test Participation

Like the downlinkers, your a/v technicians should be given a complete agenda of the program and an outline of what the system test will look and sound like. The better informed all the vendors are, the more certain you can be that each site will run smoothly.

Selecting Meeting Sites

The next chapter will go into detail on the criteria for selecting sites for your videoconference. However, the meeting room is a part of your network, so it seems reasonable here to at least lay out the technical considerations for selecting a site. These are straightforward: (1) You must be able to see the portion of the sky where your selected satellite is orbiting; and (2) if you are using C-band, the site must be free of microwave interference.

To determine both these conditions, unless the downlinker you are using has done work at the site before, have each site surveyed. Do the survey far enough in advance of the program that you will have time to change sites if any problems are discovered.

One more hint: If you are using C-band, you should do the survey at the time of day that the program will be aired. It is possible for a site to be perfectly clear during some hours and full of interference at others.

SCRAMBLING

Should you scramble or not is a matter of how secure you want your program to be. Ordering scrambling (encryption) will add about $4000 to the cost of your originating signal. Also it will add about $450 to $650 per receive site for unscrambling (decryption). The scrambling systems are combinations of electronics and computer software that must be integrated perfectly for the system to work. If some part fails to work, you can lose your whole program.

Although there have been some successes with scrambling at this writing, the systems are still not totally reliable. My advice is to steer clear of scrambling until the product improves. This means that if your message is top secret, you may not want to consider using videoconferencing.

Caroline Laden of the American Law Network, who has been deeply involved in installing and debugging an encryption system for its use, says that you need at least 30 days to get decryption equipment to local downlink vendors in an *ad hoc* network: "Scambling only adds to the confusion at sites if it is

Table 7.1: Twenty-Site Network for a Four-Hour Event

Item	Rate		Cost
Downlink, technician and system test $800	20 sites.....		$16,000
Large-screen monitor, technician 600	20 sites.....		12,000
Backup projection unit 300	20 sites.....		6,000
Audio system........................ 150	20 sites.....		3,000
Meeting room........................ 200	20 sites.....		4,000
Satellite time (C-band) .... 300 hr	4 hrs.......		1,200
Uplink time.......................... 150 hr	4 hrs.......		600
Microwave to the uplink .... 250 hr	4 hrs.......		1,000
	TOTAL		$43,800

added at the last minute. If I were doing a videoconference for the first time, I wouldn't worry about scrambling. It's an added aggravation, and you'll have enough to do." She also points out that the systems are not completely tamper-proof. "If [you announce your plans to scramble] too far in advance, those who want to steal can still steal."

Scrambling, just like every other part of the network, must have an effective backup. Laden says that you should set up a procedure to bypass the scramblers easily rather than ruin the entire broadcast if the scrambling system does not work.

This, apparently, is the only viable backup for scrambling at this point. But beware. Judy Masserang of EDS remembers the time an encryption system simply would not work. The client opted to go on the air anyway, unsecured, with a message that should never have been given access into backyard dishes. The result was an unhappy client who felt pressured to broadcast regardless of the lack of security because of all the money put into other elements of the program and network.

SAMPLE NETWORK BUDGET

The budget outlined in Table 7.1 gives you an idea of what you can expect to pay for the network portion of a videoconference. Add this to your production total, and you have the cost of a total videoconference. The budget assumes a realistic 20-city network using hotel meeting rooms to seat about 50 people each. The entire broadcast is figured to last four hours, including satellite time for testing.

CHECKLIST

Following is a checklist of the major tasks associated with setting up a network. You may find additional tasks that will relate to your individual network, but this should serve as a guide. Assuming that all decisions have been made regarding choice of cities within the network, duration of program and transmission method (C- or Ku-band), the tasks associated with networking include the following:

1.——Call satellite broker and order transponder time.
2.——Call meeting sites to reserve meeting space.
   a. Inquire as to each site's experience with videoconferencing.
   b. Prepare to phone second- and third-choice sites if the first is not available.
3.——Call downlinkers.
   a. Be prepared to tell them the name and address of the meeting site and a contact at the site.
   b. Be prepared to tell them which satellite and transponder you will be using.
   c. Ask if they can also provide a/v. If not, ask them to recommend a competent person with whom they have worked in the past.
   d. Set up a date for a site survey if needed.
4.——Call a/v dealers to order desired equipment.
   a. Be prepared to tell them the name and address of the meeting site and a contact at the site.
   b. Tell them which downlinking company you will be using.
5.——Mail confirmation forms to all vendors (a/v, downlinkers, meeting site personnel) outlining services ordered and the price agreed upon.
   a. Ask for return of signed agreement within one week.
6.——Speak with all vendors at least weekly to be certain that the project is still on track with them.
7.——Order uplink time.
8.——Order any additional connections required to access the uplink.

9.——Two weeks before air date mail instructions to downlinkers and a/v dealers.
   a. Identify the satellite and transponder.
   b. Supply times (Eastern) of system test and start of program.
   c. Specify the time they are required to be on site.
   d. List the phone number to call upon arrival at the site.
   e. List the phone number to call at start of system test.
   f. Give the name of the contact at the origination site.
   g. List the backup phone number at origination site.
   h. Specify the system test procedures.
   i. Supply the name of the client site captain/host contact.
   j. Supply the name of the meeting site contact.
10.——Two days before the event, call each vendor to confirm the services.
11.——The day before the event, call each vendor again. This time get the name and home phone number of the technician assigned to the job; also get a supervisor's name and phone number.

SUMMARY

To ensure the smooth integration of your network, tackle the steps involved one at a time. Before ordering any services, be certain to know what you need and when you'll need it. Then, don't hesitate to demand exactly the type of equipment you need at a price that is reasonable. Be sure, though, to follow up all equipment and service orders in writing to avoid any unpleasant last-minute surprises.

8

Meeting Site Considerations

It is not enough to deliver a clean satellite signal to technicians. The setting in which the videoconference is received is critical to your client's satisfaction with the event. Since the videoconference manager is unlikely to be able to visit and get to know each meeting site in a network, it is important to understand what you can expect at various sites and how to get what you want over the phone.

This chapter explores the options available in meeting sites and the considerations involved in selecting a particular site for a videoconference as well as how to use local site facilitators to keep it operating smoothly.

You must be sure that the site meets the needs of the event. This is true from several aspects: the actual physical space available, the ambience of the facility, the willingness of the staff to work well over the phone and its experience with videoconferencing.

It would be nice if there were truly a standard meeting site network available but, as Caroline Laden emphasizes, there is "such a range of facilities that standardization is difficult." This wide range exists even in hotels that market themselves as equipped for videoconferencing. The range applies to the quality of the facilities themselves and the attitudes and experience of the personnel. Judy Masserang says, "Some hotels are good at videoconferencing. For others it is just another meeting."

It will be your job as manager of your videoconference to make the most of the good meeting sites and to coax the others into taking your videoconference needs seriously.

THE ROLE OF THE MEETING PLANNER

Corporate meeting planners can be of real help in planning your videoconference. They are the people within your organization who have the most expertise in dealing with personnel at meeting sites and with making arrangements for the wide variety of services you may need at each one. These services include food and beverage, sleeping rooms, breakout meeting rooms, audiovisual facilities for supplemental sales presentations, etc.

However, meeting planners are often reluctant to get involved in or endorse videoconferencing. Some see satellite events as a threat to the traditional types of meetings that gain them travel to exotic locations to arrange conventions and motivational trips. The reality is, however, that gatherings like that are unlikely to be replaced by videoconferencing. Try to enlist the support of your company's meeting planner. This may involve explaining that you are providing your company with an additional tool, not a replacement for anything the planner has been doing. It will be to the planner's advantage, in the long run, to add videoconference expertise to his or her bag of tricks.

TYPES OF SITES

The type of site you choose is entirely dependent upon the needs of your event. Caroline Laden chooses the sites for American Law Network videoconferences with the following criteria in mind: (1) They must be downtown, near the lawyer population; (2) they must be convenient for the attendees and have parking and food service; and (3) they must be conducive to the educational process. (see Figure 8.1.)

You must examine the purpose of your videoconference, define who the expected audience will be and determine the mode of transportation that you expect most attendees to use. (For instance, if most will be driving, you will need an easily accessible site with ample parking.) Then you are ready to decide what type of facility you will need. As mentioned earlier, due to the availability of transportable downlinks, the network can be made up of almost any type of site you choose or it may be a combination of many different types. (See Figure 8.2.) The most commonly used sites will be discussed here.

Figure 8.1: Attorneys participating in an educational seminar delivered via satellite to receive site, part of the American Law Network. Photo courtesy COMSAT General Corp.

Figure 8.2: Receive site at the U.S. Chamber of Commerce in Washington, DC. Photo courtesy Associated Builders and Contractors, Inc.

Hotels

Hotel sites are most often chosen for videoconference networks. This is true for several reasons:

1. Hotels are equipped with meeting space.
2. Some hotel chains (e.g., Holiday Inns, Inc. and Marriott Corp.) have a great deal of experience with videoconferencing and may even have all the technical equipment you need on site.
3. Hotels offer food and beverage service.
4. Hotels supply rooms for overnight guests.
5. Most hotels have some parking facilities.
6. Most hotels offer brochures and maps to make it easy for out-of-town attendees to find them.

There are some things to watch out for, though, when dealing with hotels for your videoconference.

In most cases, a videoconference is not an extremely important piece of business for them. They place videoconferencing in the same category as weddings and local club dinners because you will probably use only a limited amount of their space, your attendees will be in and out quickly, and it is unlikely that you will use many overnight rooms or need much food service. Hotels make their money first from sleeping rooms and second from food and beverage sales. They would much rather book a week-long convention that guarantees blocks of sleeping rooms and many full meals. This fact of life does not leave you with much negotiating power unless you can arrange to have your videoconference become part of a much larger function.

The long and short of it is that, since your business is not critical to the hotel, you may find it difficult to command the attention you may need from individual personnel. That is why it is important to have a good local meeting captain, an employee of the end user who resides in the meeting site city and who is willing to act as a persistent and effective local contact.

Hotels often change personnel. You may find yourself being shunted from person to person throughout your project. This can waste your time and cause you frustration as you find yourself explaining your project over and over again to people who do not understand videoconferencing clearly.

Hotels sometimes make booking errors. We found ourselves on one occasion being told at the last minute, "Sorry, but we made an error in booking, and we can't let you have your space." That may be all right for a local lodge meeting, but it will hardly do when you are putting on a costly national sales event. Be certain that you verify and double-verify that the space is, indeed, yours to use and that no other group has a prior hold on it that supersedes your claim.

Catering prices at hotels can sometimes be shocking. We once ordered "dry snacks" as part of an open bar for a client, fully expecting a complete range of goodies like nuts, crackers and cheese. After all, the quoted price had been $80 for a party of under 30 people. The dry snacks turned out to be one bowl of potato chips. The lesson here, which we learned the hard way, is: Get everything in writing. Every snack, every drink, every entrée, every side dish—and their prices—should be guaranteed in writing well in advance of the function.

Another word about catering at the receive sites. Emphasize to the hotel that you cannot have a variance in the timing of coffee breaks. During an ordinary meeting, if the coffee service arrives ten minutes too early or too late, no one even notices. But in a videoconference, at which every break will be timed to the minute, a late coffee break can create havoc, especially with a large audience. We have found that hotels are quite willing to accommodate this need for timing. Just explain why it's important and you should expect full cooperation.

Hotels often fail to take seriously an order for a telephone in the meeting room. You must have a phone to use for the system test and for the Q&A session. Even though a jack may be in place, and even though you have indicated in writing—and have gotten agreement from the hotel—that you absolutely require a phone, count on it—it will not be there on the morning of the event. Why? My guess is that a phone is such a small detail to a busy hotel staff that it slips through the cracks. Just be certain that your meeting captain is advised to expect the problem.

Hotels, as a rule, do not have the most convenient phone systems for Q&A use. In most hotels the phone line that goes into the meeting room must pass through the main switchboard. Sometimes it is even necessary to speak with the hotel operator before getting an outside line to make a long-distance call. This can be a nuisance if you expect to make a large number of calls from your meeting room phone. However, most videoconferences require that only two or three phone calls be placed to the originating site throughout the event.

If you think the switchboard routine could be a problem for you, you can have a direct line installed in the hotel meeting room (some busy hotels require this). Call the local telephone company to arrange for this. Expect to pay $250 or so for the service. Be sure to order the phone as early as possible, as the paperwork from the phone company can be formidable, and it's rare that you will find hotel personnel knowledgeable enough to smooth the way.

Hotels have limited facilities for storing and keeping track of preshipped materials. If your conference requires that you pre-ship books or cartons of product, be certain before making meeting space arrangements that the hotel can handle it. If it can, be sure to ship only to your hotel contact so that the materials don't get lost or shoved into an inappropriate corner because the hotel's receiving department does not know what to do with them.

Procter & Gamble videoconferences sometimes require the preshipment of product and other materials. In order to be sure that everything has arrived and is accounted for, the planners place a unique serial number on each box and address the shipment to the hotel contact. The person in charge at the hotel is then asked over the phone to read off the serial numbers on the boxes that have arrived. This assures P&G that everything is accounted for. Previously, when serial numbers were not asked for, hotel personnel were likely to be quite careless about the shipment and reply, "Oh, sure, we have it," even though the complete shipment had not arrived.

Prices at hotels vary widely. We have paid as little as $75 for a room at a fine hotel to seat over a hundred people and as much as $1000 at other sites for the same size room. Each site is unique in its pricing. You can expect the best prices if you are hitting a hotel in a slow business period or if you plan some sort of extensive food function. A simple coffee break will not account for much. But if you plan a complete sit-down meal, ask—and expect to get—a waiver of meeting room charges.

Campus Sites

Some colleges are already part of established networks, such as National University Teleconferencing Network (NUTN), whose headquarters are at Oklahoma State University in Stillwater, OK. It was set up to deliver additional educational opportunities to its members. The sites are usually available to corporate users for a fee. However, bear in mind that the first priority of the college is to provide education for its students. Earning money from renting their videoconferencing facilities is really only a fringe benefit in their budgets. That means that anything of an educational nature, even though it may earn no money for the college, will probably have first crack at the facilities. On the other hand, there are several nice things about using college campuses as receive sites:

1. Campuses that are equipped to receive videoconferences usually provide a complete package including downlink, audiovisual equipment, technicians and meeting space.
2. The meeting space is often in an established, comfortable auditorium.
3. The ambience of a college campus can be quite pleasant.
4. Food service, although generally not of gourmet quality, is usually available through the company that runs the cafeteria.
5. The price is right. Expect to pay about $1000 to $2000 for everything for a full day.

There are, though, some things that are not so good at college campuses:

1. The equipment is often operated by students. Their inexperience can be a real problem. Check to see that they are at least supervised by a full-time professional.
2. The low price at colleges sometimes grows to a high price. You can find yourself having extra, totally unexpected fees added. For example, at a campus receive site for a recent program, we found that the college required the presence of a security guard since outsiders were on the grounds. That cost $25 an hour. Then we found that, since we were using electricity, union rules required the presence from setup through teardown of an electrician. Another $25 an hour. There were other minor charges, too, that caused that site to be one of the most expensive in our network. However, this is not true at all campuses. Just be sure you know what the total will be before you agree to the site.
3. There are usually no public sleeping accommodations on campuses. If rooms are required, ask about hotels within a reasonable distance of the campus.
4. Parking can be a problem. Most campuses have acres of parking space, but this is primarily space reserved and paid for by faculty and students. Unauthorized cars in such spaces may even be towed away. Check with your contact at the college. It may be possible to get one-day

parking passes for your attendees. Or, if the event falls on a weekend or evening, you may be able to have one full lot blocked off for your use.

Public Television Stations

Public television stations, through the PBS system, made up the first real network of videoconference receive sites. This is because the PBS system itself was the first TV network to be delivered by satellite. PBS staffers found out early that the satellite system available to them was an effective way to communicate with the many far-flung stations in the system. This use of the network was later expanded and offered for a fee to educational groups, then corporations.

The primary role for public television stations is to bring programming into the homes of their local viewers. It takes money to do this. With the funds from government sources decreasing dramatically over the past several years, public television stations looked hard at ways to bring cash into the till. They all had satellite receive equipment and most of them already had meeting space. They quickly figured out that combining the two assets could allow them to sell their services as videoconference meeting facilities.

First, here are some positive aspects of using public television stations:

1. The price is often lower than at hotels. You can expect to pay from $500 to $2000 a day to use their facilities. However, be cautious; some stations charge by the hour. When they say $500, they may mean per hour, and a full day's videoconference can get very expensive at that rate.

2. The equipment you need, and qualified technicians to run it, are already at the site.

3. The PBS system has a department in Alexandria, VA, called ConferSat (part of PBS Enterprises) to help you book suitable space at stations, thus saving you a lot of legwork. However, the usual up-front fee of a couple of thousand dollars for researching the availability of con-

ference sites is not refundable even though you decide not to use the PBS network.

There are additional things to be aware of in booking public television receive sites:

1. Many stations use a studio as a meeting room. Often the facilities consist of metal folding chairs set up in a row on a concrete floor in a room that is hypercooled. Ask about the seating before you sign.
2. Parking is sometimes a problem since many public television stations are in the center of town.
3. Some public television stations are in neighborhoods that are clearly unsafe after dark. Before booking, call someone you know in that city to ask about the location.
4. Although public television stations gladly arrange for catering, about the most you can expect is a buffet that will be served in the same cold studio.
5. Of course, no sleeping accommodations are available at the studios themselves and, because of the location of most of these stations, they may also not be available nearby.

Hospital Networks

Several networks of hospitals have been established to allow programming to be delivered directly to busy medical staff. Although there are dozens of these networks working autonomously, most of their facilities can be booked through the Association of Hospital Television Networks in Pittsburgh, PA, or Voluntary Hospitals of America in Irving, TX.

These networks deliver educational material to staff, and entertainment to patients, and they sometimes carry data or phone calls for a complete hospital network. If you are delivering programming of a strictly educational nature aimed at nurses or doctors, this is the network for you. And if you meet the above criteria, the cost is *low*. It varies from nothing to only a couple of hundred dollars.

The bad part is that you must meet the above criteria or you cannot take advantage of this system.

Regardless of the type of network you choose, be sure to specify in advance exactly what services you will require and what you have agreed to pay for those services. A form is included in the appendix that can be used to detail all services and prices. This should be mailed to the meeting site for authorization and then returned to you.

DETERMINING SPACE REQUIREMENTS

One of the services to be confirmed is the meeting room itself and its dimensions. Here are the minimum requirements you will need in your videoconference room:

- chairs to accommodate your audience, staggered for easy viewing
- a screen in the front of the room for the projection system
- a table in the back of the room that will hold a telephone
- a table to hold materials
- a podium or lectern at the front of the room

When you make your call to the meeting facility, specify very clearly how much space you need. An excellent aid for determining space requirements is a tool called *The Arranger,* available for a small fee from Meeting Planners International of Dallas, TX. *The Arranger* is a simple sliderule-like tool that tells you how many square feet you must have to seat an audience of a certain size in a certain configuration (i.e., theater style, classroom style, etc.).

Add six to eight feet in the front of the room to accommodate front-screen video projection equipment. Try not to use rear-screen projection in a typical hotel meeting room because it takes up too much valuable space. However, you will probably find rear-screen already installed in college auditoriums, and that's fine, because they have the space to accommodate it behind the stage.

Have your meeting site contact tell you which room you will

be in. Your satellite technician will have to know this in order to perform a meaningful site survey. If you are going to use transportable satellite receive equipment, keep in mind that the meeting room should be as close as possible to the lot where the downlink will be parked. There must also be an easy way for the downlink technician to run a cable from the room to the downlink.

Ask the meeting site contact about obstructions in the room. Ask about poles and low-hanging chandeliers. After all, a videoconference is pointless if the audience can't see the presentation.

Don't let personnel at the meeting site talk you into a room that will be too small for you. If your minimum space requirements are not available, go elsewhere. Otherwise your audience will be uncomfortable, with the people in the back row craning their necks to see the screen.

Which brings me to one more point. If you expect more than four rows of audience, ask the hotel to provide a riser in the front of the room so you can elevate the screen a couple of feet. Of course, this requires that the ceiling be high enough to allow it. Ask your contact. The comfort of the receive site is crucial to the success of your videoconference.

SITE CAPTAINS

Site captains, sometimes called site facilitators or meeting captains, can be an important ingredient in ensuring the success of your event.

An ideal site captain will be a regular employee of the client with enough clout to make decisions and with a real interest in the success of the program. Site captains who are not as ideal can be hired from employment agencies that specialize in temporary services, but they are not recommended because they will not have the same interest in a successful event as your client's own employee will.

The captains should reside in the cities for whose sites they are responsible. As soon as you know which meeting facilities will be used, inform the local site captain of the site, its address and the name of the contact person. Ask the captain to visit the site and meet the contact. This personal attention will go a long way toward gaining cooperation from meeting facility personnel. The captain should also be the main contact for local meal functions. Even though you may be lining up the basic food services, let the local people pick the menu. Visiting the site and selecting a menu will take only an hour or two of the captain's time but will improve the site satisfaction of the entire group.

Site captains should also be responsible for arriving at the site early on the day of the event to check to see that the room has been arranged correctly and that all equipment has been set up and is running. They should corroborate those facts in the call to the origination site during the system test.

Sometimes the site captain is also designated as the only person at a site who may phone questions in to the origination point during the Q&A, but this more or less depends on how you have chosen to handle the entire Q&A procedure.

One warning. Make clear to the site captains what, if any, additional services they may order at the meeting facility on their own. If they are permitted to order added services, be sure that both they and the hotel staff are clear as to all billing procedures. One central billing point to which bills, receipts and detailed descriptions of all services are sent will make accounting easier after the event.

SITE FACILITATOR'S GUIDE

Each meeting captain should receive well in advance of the event a complete facilitator's guide. This may entail anything from one page to a full manual, depending upon the complexity of your program.

The facilitator's guide should include everything the captain needs to know about the program:

- hotel contact name and phone number
- expected room setup
- expected audiovisual equipment
- expected time for room and a/v setup to be completed
- name of downlink technician
- name of audiovisual technician

- time of system test
- how to respond during system test
- what to do in case of emergency
- how to handle the Q&A
- schedule of events (food functions, receptions, breakout seminars, etc.)
- names and phone numbers to call at origination site with questions on the day of the event
- names and phone numbers to call with questions before the event

Send along with the facilitator's guide a packet of evaluation forms for distribution by the meeting captain after the event. (More about evaluation in the next chapter.)

Your event may require even more information. The guide must be written especially for the site in order to be helpful to your site captain. A sample site facilitator's guide is included in the appendix as an example of one prepared for a recent videoconference.

Keep in touch with both your site captain and your meeting facility contact in the days and weeks before the event. The more information they have, the more they will understand the event and the importance of their roles. Complete understanding will help avoid costly and embarrassing errors.

SUMMARY

Many types of meeting sites are available for use in a videoconference network because of the availability of transportable downlinks. Your local satellite technician can survey the site that you prefer to be sure that it is in a location where it is possible to receive signals from a satellite. Once you get the all clear for reception, your other concerns will be more mundane but just as critical to the success of your event. These involve arranging for adequate meeting space and other needed services. Your site captain can be a real help in monitoring receive locations in distant cities.

9

Managing the Project

This chapter emphasizes the importance of tight project management. At this point you have seen what is in store for you in planning a videoconference. The word *planning* has been emphasized again and again. Not only do you need a good plan, you need a method of keeping it on track.

PROJECT MANAGEMENT

Project management is more often thought to belong to the world of large construction and equipment installation projects. However, those same techniques are invaluable in any project that involves many parts and a fair amount of complexity.

Here are the principles behind project management:

1. Set a realistic timetable for completing the project.
2. Identify the tasks that must be done to complete the project.
3. Identify those tasks that are contingent upon the completion of earlier tasks.
4. Assign specific tasks to specific people.
5. Assign completion deadlines to each individual task.
6. Set up a system of checkpoints to aid in keeping the project on schedule.

Setting A Timetable

In setting up a timetable for a project, it is best to work backward from the target completion date. This helps clarify your thinking as you realize, for example, that before you go on air you must rehearse your talent, but before you rehearse your talent you must have a script, etc. Even if you have not been given an exact deadline, set one of your own to give yourself a framework in which to operate.

Setting a deadline helps to define and narrow your tasks more clearly. A good example of this is apparent in the field of writing and research. An author with no deadline is tempted to go on forever, never completing the book because there is always one more fact to research or one more sentence to polish. However, the author with a tight deadline works more effectively, containing the research to the realistically obtainable. Videoconference projects are no different.

Before setting a complete timetable, though, you will need a good grasp of the tasks to be accomplished as well as the length of time that they should take to complete. Unless you are an expert in every phase of videoconferencing, get the input of everyone who will be involved in the project before you set your timetable. These people are the ones who will have to live within the time constraints, and they should be happier with limitations that they have set themselves.

Identifying Tasks

Break down the jobs to be accomplished first into major tasks like "complete scripts," "build set." Once these have been defined in the logical order in which they should be completed, break each general category down into its component tasks. The task list for "complete scripts" would look like this:

1. Assign writers.
2. Select script topics.
3. Define script timing limitations.
4. Write first draft.
5. Review first draft.
6. Rewrite script.
7. Get final approval of script.

Contingent Tasks

It is important, too, to understand which tasks must be

completed before others can be begun. If these contingencies are built into your plan, you will save some time and maybe even some money. For example, there is no point in calling your satellite downlinkers for service until you know, for sure, where your receive sites are going to be. Calling the downlinkers first will mean that you will need to call them a second time with the meeting site address. This will waste your time and the cost of a phone call. Always try to make your tasks as efficient as possible to cut down on unnecessary personnel time and expense.

Assigning Tasks

Once the tasks have been defined, assign them to people with experience in performing them. These people should need little supervision and be able to perform their functions with only the guidance of your clear definition and your set deadline.

Once you have developed and laid out your complete project timetable, give copies to all involved. These timetables will help them understand where their tasks fit in and will graphically demonstrate their deadlines and the time period in which they are expected to make real progress, which will be checked by the project's manager.

Assigning Deadlines

Deadlines are, of course, contingent upon the overall time frame of the project. If the time for the overall project is short, naturally everyone will need to put some extra effort into completing the task in a shorter period of time. And these will be the same people who had input into defining these tasks, so they should be at least somewhat comfortable about the deadlines.

Oddly enough, one thing to be wary of is a timetable that is too long. People tend to get into the spirit of working long and hard together on a job with a close deadline. But stretch that deadline out, and the urgency of the situation disappears. Stretch it too far, and your colleagues may even forget they were ever assigned a task, missing deadlines altogether. So if you do have the luxury of a long timeline, tighten up your management controls and increase your vigilance at checkpoints to be sure that nothing slips.

Setting Checkpoints

As you develop your timetable, set definite dates for checking progress. With a fairly long timetable, these may fall once a week. There may be a need for a checkpoint once a day if your time is particularly short.

The reason for checking is to be absolutely certain that the project is ontime. If one person is having a problem completing task A, you are then in a position to find some help rather than let task B, contingent upon the completion of task A, slip. Emphasize to those working on the project that the idea behind checkpoints is not to be insulting or punitive, but rather to be certain that help is given where needed in a timely manner.

Table 9.1 is a sample timetable for a fictitious videoconference project that has been assigned two months before air date. This chart is meant to be a guide in laying out your own timetable. As a guide it is not meant to be all-inclusive. Not all of the minor tasks to be accomplished have been laid out. You, of course, will be developing your own task list to suit your project.

Once you have laid out your timetable, prepare a task assignment chart to be used at checkpoint meetings. This chart will record every task, the person to whom the task has been assigned and the progress to be made on the task within a specified time.

At each checkpoint meeting, use the recorded chart from the previous meeting to note completion (or noncompletion) of the task. Use a fresh chart for each checkpoint meeting. File these charts. After your project is completed they can be a valuable tool in helping you refine your management of the next event. See Table 9.2 for a sample checkpoint chart.

Always arrive at these checkpoint meetings with a well-planned agenda, which you follow. This will maximize the productivity of your meetings and will serve as an example of good organization for your videoconference team.

Table 9.1: Videoconference Timetable
Air Date = October 1

TASK	8/6	8/13	8/20	8/27	9/3	9/10	9/17	9/24	9/30	10/1
Choose city network	X									
Determine audience size	X									
Decide on type of site	X									
Determine seating style	X									
Reserve meeting rooms	X	X								
Hire downlinkers		X	X							
Hire a/v personnel		X	X							
Plan production	X		X							
Assign script writers			X							
Assign script details			X							
Write first draft			X	X						
Review draft				X						
Complete scripts				X	X					
Get management approval for scripts						X				
Select a studio			X	X						
Design set			X	X						

Table 9.1 (continued)

TASK	8/6	8/13	8/20	8/27	9/3	9/10	9/17	9/24	9/30	10/1
Build set							X	X		
Prepare graphics						X		X		
Prepare tele-prompter copy								X	X	
Hold technical rehearsal									X	
Hold dress rehearsal									X	
Reserve satellite time				X						
Reserve uplink time				X						
Perform site surveys				X	X					
Mail confirmation to all vendors					X					
Receive confirmation from vendors							X			
Assign meeting captains				X						
Mail site details to meeting captains						X				
Select menu							X			

Table 9.1 (continued)

TASK	8/6	8/13	8/20	8/27	9/3	9/10	9/17	9/24	9/30	10/1
Make follow-up calls to vendors						X		X	X	X	
Mail technical information to vendors									X		
Write site facilitator's guide							X	X			
Mail site facilitator's guide									X		
Check last-minute details										X	
On air											X

Table 9.2 SAMPLE CHECKPOINT CHART

Task	Task To Be Done	Person Responsible	Target Date	Completion Date
Write script	First draft	Susan B.	May 15	May 14
Reserve sites	Confirm all sites east of Mississippi R.	Jim R.	May 5	May 5
Hire production company	Secure bids for review	Mary C.	May 10	One bid missing extension to May 14.

SUMMARY

Implementing a tight project management procedure can ensure that all of the tasks involved in putting on a videoconference event will be accomplished in a timely manner. Creating a timetable for all members of the team to follow gives the manager a great deal of control over the project and also allows all team members to better understand how their responsibilities fit in and what impact they have on the overall project.

10

Remaining in Control on the Day of the Event

The day your videoconference airs will be filled with tension and demands for last-minute decisions. If the network is to run smoothly, you must prepare well in advance for every possibility. Each detail must be planned for and all tasks must be assigned. This is the only way to avoid losing control in the hours immediately preceding air time.

The culmination of the project occurs on the day of the event. At this point all contingencies outlined in earlier chapters have been examined, and plans are in place for solving any problems that may arise. The site facilitator's guide has been in the hands of your meeting captains for several days. All vendors have had copies of the instructions for their individual sites for days. You are comfortable that everyone in the network understands his or her role.

The importance of the preparation that has preceded this day will become evident as expected problems occur and are solved and as unexpected problems are handled with presence of mind.

The unexpected will occur. Clare Mann says that unexpected problems tend to shock people because we all are inclined to think that "in this high-tech age everything works. It doesn't."

Judy Masserang of EDS remembers that early in her career she had her worst networking disaster. It was strictly a series of unexpected problems—the network lost 6 downlinks out of 23 due to unrelated local technical problems. The lesson she learned is that "this is just technology." All anyone can do is plan as well as possible.

When the event day arrives, you may be surrounded by people in a state of panic. That is why you must be prepared to remain in control. Someone must be if the process is to flow in an orderly fashion. The state of panic is natural. It is akin to the jitters felt in a theatrical production just before the curtain goes up. The client will be on edge. The talent will be nervous. And—count on it—something will go wrong, giving even you cause for alarm unless you are prepared.

The ideal, of course, would be for everything to work smoothly and on time, for there to be no technical errors and for the talent to be prepared, at ease and "professional."

Two professionals in the business have their own techniques for remaining in control—a little something added after all the careful planning. Len Aulenbach of SmithKline says this little something extra is very important. What is it? Prayer, according to Len. He is not alone in feeling that the quirks of technology may threaten his control over circumstances. Clare Mann has a customary prayer that he offers just before going on air: "Please, God, let the signal end up somewhere besides up."

To be sure that you come as close as possible to the ideal, a checklist follows of preparations that will have been made a few days before the event. Then, a complete outline of a typical videoconference day should complete your preparation for your own event.

When you arrive at the studio or other production location, you should have the following with you:

1. at least one assistant who can leave the phone control center to locate people or things that you need. Plan to have another assistant arrive shortly thereafter who can serve to greet talent, guests and VIPs.
2. a schedule—*to the minute*—of the day's events
3. a list of *everyone* involved in the project at the production site. Include times of arrival and roles for the following:
   a. production crew
   b. caterers

c. reception personnel
d. client support personnel
e. talent
f. telephone operators
g. audience members
h. others as appropriate
4. names and phone numbers of all outside vendors:
   a. caterers
   b. meeting site contact personnel and backup personnel at all receive sites
   c. audiovisual personnel, their backups and their supervisors for all receive sites
   d. downlink technicians and their backups for all receive sites
   e. uplinker
   f. satellite time broker and operations center
   g. microwave connection vendors
   h. temporary personnel and their backups at each site, who may be used as hosts or ticket takers
   i. security personnel at all sites if setup requires entry into meeting facilities in off hours
5. a list of all services ordered for all sites
6. a list of the names of the meeting rooms at all sites and the numbers of the phone extensions in those rooms
7. procedures for phone operators to use during the system test
8. procedures to be used for the question-and-answer part of the program
9. home phone numbers for any colleagues important to the event. You may need to contact them long before they arrive at the office. Also their office numbers and extensions along with the names of their secretaries
10. a copy of the site facilitator's guide
11. 4 x 6 (or 3 x 5) cards for incoming questions
12. pens or pencils
13. a list of all sites to be used for recording check-in and comments during the system test
14. the name and number—including home number—of the

vendor who supplied the phones at the origination site for Q&A and system test
15. a schedule of programming that will be aired on the satellite transponder assigned to you during the three hours preceding the start of your system test
16. technical information such as identification of transponder, satellite and audio channels to be used for your event

EVENT SCHEDULE

The tasks related to the day of your event will be unique. However, most videoconferences have many elements in common. The following schedule represents a typical videoconference day and is meant to serve as a guide in setting your own expectations. It outlines what should happen, what could go wrong and how to avoid problems. The sample does not cover specific concerns related to the television production portion itself since those were covered in an earlier chapter, and at this point the production per se is out of your hands. Your hands will be full as it is.

We'll assume that your event is a two-hour videoconference scheduled to air at 11:00 a.m. Eastern Time. This means that the start is 10:00 a.m. in the Central Time zone, 9:00 a.m. in the Mountain Time zone, and 8:00 a.m. in the Pacific Time zone. All times in the schedule are Eastern.

One Day Prior to the Event

11:00 a.m.

If you are using a transportable uplink, it—and its engineer—should be on hand 24 hours before the start of your event. The delivery and setup of equipment as ponderous and complex as an uplink holds promise of many potential problems. Allow plenty of time to solve these problems. If you are using a fixed uplink, this part need not concern you.

The following are things to think about regarding a transportable uplink:

- Consider your transport. The uplink itself will probably be delivered via tractor trailer truck over our nation's often perilous highway system. *Expect* something to happen. A flat tire or bad weather can cause serious delays. At worst, an accident could occur that would make the uplink totally inoperable. A 24-hour window will give you time to secure another uplink or to arrange for emergency access via microwave or landlines.
- Have your engineer there early. Putting off the engineer's arrival until the last minute can be risky. Anyone can be delayed by bad weather. Allowing 24 hours gives time for waiting in airports or making the decision to drive or take a bus. Another factor here is that something, perhaps something minor, could easily be damaged during the transport of the uplink. Getting your engineer on site early will give time to correct problems. It will also give time for getting to know the crew and the equipment at the production site, which will help ensure the smooth transmission of the event.
- Go over the technical requirements of the site. With 24 hours almost anything can be solved. A malfunctioning audio line into the uplink truck, for example, could be a disaster an hour before the event, but it becomes an easily handled problem when enough time is allowed to connect and test all signal and power sources.

2:00 p.m.

Be sure the phones that will be used for Q&A and the system test are operational. If they are not, this early test will allow you to contact your phone vendor for emergency correction.

End of Day

Before leaving, be sure that your name and your assistants' names appear on the appropriate list so that security personnel will be able to let you in early the next morning.

The Day of the Event

5:00 a.m.

You and your assistants arrive at the production site. Make a quick visual check to be sure that everything appears to be in order. Proceed to the room where the phones have been placed for incoming calls to the network. Place all materials as outlined in the checklist above in an easily accessible spot.

Check the phones. Be certain you can get a dial tone and make an outgoing call. Have a colleague call you back on the published Q&A number to be sure it is working. Have the colleague call you several times with various phones off the hook to be sure that the hunt capability of your system is working. If any part of the phone system is malfunctioning, call your phone system supplier at home. Don't hesitate to call at any hour: the phones are too important to you.

Check the monitor in the phone room. It should be installed and operational. This monitor may be the only direct link you will have with the production itself.

6:00 a.m.

(Remember, this means 5:00 a.m. Central, 4:00 a.m. Mountain and 3:00 a.m. Pacific.) Audiovisual and downlink technicans arrive at their assigned meeting sites. They are to call you upon arrival. Check off their locations as they call. Note any problems that they may encounter at their sites. Should you not hear from these people by 6:15 a.m., call the meeting site to track them down. If they can't be found on site, call their backups' numbers or their supervisors' numbers to assure that the assigned backup person is dispatched immediately. Ask the backup person to call upon arrival at the site.

7:00 a.m.

All audiovisual and downlink personnel are to be set up and ready. Although you will not be broadcasting yet, in most cases some other programming will appear on the transponder that you are scheduled to use. Your downlinkers can use that programming to be certain that they have focused on the correct transponder and to make adjustments to their equipment. The audiovisual vendor can have that equipment set up, tested and cabled to the downlink to assure clear reception from your transponder. If no programming is scheduled to appear on the transponder to be used at this time of day, be sure the audiovisual technician has a videotape player to allow for adequate testing of the equipment.

These technicians will have been instructed to place a call to you at this time reporting that (a) all is well (b) some minor adjustments have yet to be made, along with a description of those adjustments or (c) there has been a major failure.

If all is well, suggest that the technicians relax over some breakfast and come back at about 8:30 (Eastern, remember) to prepare for the system test. Be sure, though, that someone is left guarding the equipment or that they lock the door before leaving.

If all is not well, ask them to call every 15 minutes with an update on progress. And don't panic. Remember that this is why you are paying for redundant equipment. Vendors should have a spare of everything—from cables to connectors to monitors to receivers—in case something goes wrong. They should be instructed to swap troublesome equipment for the backup as soon as it becomes clear that the problem will not be easily solved. This will save both you and them from undue anxiety.

Also, by 7:00 a.m. all crew and technical personnel will have arrived at the production location. Be sure they immediately check out all equipment and keep you advised of any last-minute problems. Why? You will be the one to authorize outside services if needed.

One more thing should happen by 7:00 a.m. A caterer should arrive with coffee, tea, juice and rolls for crew, talent, phone operators and management personnel. This will go a long way toward keeping everyone cheerful and will prevent the loss of important personnel as they "run out for a cup of coffee."

8:00 a.m.

Place a call to uplink (if not on site), microwave or other interconnection company, if any, and satellite operations center to double-check on all arrangements and to ascertain if there are any problems at their ends that you should be aware of.

8:30 a.m.

Some of your phone operators will arrive to help with the system test. Have an assistant greet them at the door, check their names off a prepared list, hang up their coats and escort them to the phone room.

For each five sites, plan on one system test operator. Provide each of them with written instructions on handling the system test. Have plenty of pens and 4 x 6 (or 3 x 5) cards available for them to take notes. Explain the procedure they have just read and answer their questions. Take off the hook all phones that are not attended by an operator.

Meeting captains are to arrive at all meeting sites at this time and use their previously provided checklists to assure that all is in order.

If this is a pay-per-view event, the personnel will arrive at the receive sites for selling tickets and distributing programs. These people will report to the meeting captains from whom they will receive final instructions, cash for change, tickets, programs and other materials as needed. These personnel will check to be sure that a table or booth has been placed in a prominent position for ticket sales. If this is missing or inadequate, the meeting captain is to call upon the designated meeting site contact for correction.

9:00 a.m.

System test begins. The procedures to be followed during the test itself by production and receive site personnel will have been established several days before the event and published in the site facilitator's guide. These procedures now kick into place with the start of transmission from your location that features a predetermined message alerting technicians and meeting captains that the test has begun and it is time to call the system test number.

The phones should begin to ring. When they do, the answering operator will first ask the name of the site from which the call is coming, then the name of the caller. The caller will be asked if video is being received, if audio is clear, if the phone in the meeting room (from which they should be calling) is operational and if they perceive any problems at the site. They will also be asked about the presence of temporary ticket personnel if this is a pay-per-view event.

When a site is called in as all clear, check it off your list. Instruct the operator to turn the call over to you if problems are reported. Ascertain the nature of the problem. If it is generated by your origination site, turn it over to the engineers dealing with the uplink or production. If the problem is local, find out what is being done to fix it and ask the meeting captain for an update every 15 minutes until it is resolved. If you do not think the problem is being handled well, call the supervisor of the technician at fault to dispatch either replacement equipment or an additional technician to help solve the problem IMMEDIATELY.

Some sites will not call you regardless of the emphasis you have placed on the importance of the system test. This may happen for one of several reasons: (1) the prior reception test may have signaled an all clear to the technician and the meeting captain, and they may both be out of the room when the test that requests a phone call begins; (2) they may feel so secure that they have turned off the monitor; (3) something is drastically wrong, and no signal is being received; (4) the technician or meeting captain may have forgotten to be present for the start of the test or may be busy with other matters that cause them to disregard the message on the monitor.

The first thing to do is to send a new, *flashing*, signal over the network requesting specific sites to check in. Use the meeting captains' names where possible. This will bring in the majority of missing calls. For the sites where this does not work, call the direct numbers at the offending sites. If there is no answer, call your meeting site contact (for instance, if it is a hotel, this may be the catering manager) to track down the meeting captain and technicians. They may be outside with the receive dish, in the coffee shop or just standing in the hallway outside the meeting room.

Once again, don't panic. This will be at least the third contact that you have had with each site, so you will have a good feel for status. The greatest importance of this test is to check you own signal and local interconnections. Are your video and audio clear? Has your signal reached the uplink, and is it being received by and transmitted from the satellite transponder?

9:30 a.m.

The makeup artist arrives. A room will have been designated for him or her to lay out the necessary materials and prepare for the arrival of the talent.

10:00 a.m.

Talent arrive for makeup. If more than two or three people will appear on camera, you will want to allow even more time for makeup. This can be estimated during your early production meetings. Please be sure that someone has greeted the talent at the door, hung up their coats and escorted them to the makeup room. The assistant who performs this duty must be personable and helpful and well briefed on the procedures of the day. The objective is to make your talent feel confident that everything is under control and that the entire event is in good hands. An incompetent receptionist could make them doubt the competence of the whole operation, making them apprehensive and having a negative impact on their performances.

10:15 a.m.

If your production calls for a studio audience, it should arrive at this time. Your assigned receptionists (you will need at least two to handle the stragglers among the talent and the early arrivals among the audience) will check off the names of the audience members as they arrive from the prepared list of attendees. The receptionist will show them where to hang their coats and will lead them into a holding area—a large room close by the studio. The purpose of the holding area is to be sure that all audience members have arrived before explaining any procedures with which they should be familiar and to prevent them from being underfoot as the production crew makes last-minute preparations in the studio.

10:30 a.m.

The remaining phone operators arrive. These are the additional people who will help with the phones during the question-and-answer period. Your receptionists will greet these people, check their names off the operator list, see to it that their coats and hung up and escort them to the phone room.

As soon as they are settled, explain the day's events to them in general terms and ask them to review the prepared operator instructions. Be certain that a supply of pens and cards has been provided at each phone. Review the written instructions step by step to be sure the operators know how to screen calls and record questions. Introduce to the operators the person who is to be given the written questions (or informed about the phoned-in questions if the callers are to be heard live on air) for review and delivery to the on-air talent. Turn on the monitor in the phone room, both audio and video.

10:45 a.m.

Have an assistant escort the audience members into the studio and seat them. By this time the talent will be on the set. They will have been escorted there previously by production personnel assigned that responsibility at previous rehearsals.

11:00 a.m.

On air.

At this point your only job is to sit back, watch the event on your monitor, answer any questions that may arise from the phone operators or technicians in the field and wait for the Q&A session.

The Q&A will begin with an announcement by the talent and a graphic that will be transmitted displaying the number to call. Your procedures for taking questions and delivering them to

Figure 10.1: Phone room set up to receive questions from remote sites in an area removed from the studio to assure quiet for the operators. A monitor is provided so that the operators can watch the program. Photo courtesy The Procter & Gamble Company.

the talent have been prearranged during the production planning phase of the project. Keep unnecessary personnel out of the phone room. The operators will need to hear clearly and will only be impeded by unneeded voices in the background. (See Figure 10.1.)

Expect some short time lag—a minute to five minutes— before questions begin to come in. Your meeting captains will need this time to gather questions at their receive sites and place their calls. This lag will be even longer if the meeting captains have been asked to screen all questions (or questioners) before placing calls. Once the calls begin, though, the action will be fast and furious. (see Figure 10.2.) Be alert to the needs of the operators. Be prepared to provide extra writing materials as needed. Listen to determine that the incoming calls are being handled according to procedure. Be on hand to assist with difficult calls or give guidance.

Figure 10.2: Operators taking questions from audience members at remote sites. Photo courtesy SmithKline Beckman.

Once the Q&A period is over (after a few minutes, an hour or more) the videoconference will come to an end.

1:00 p.m.

Off air.

Thank your operators and dismiss them. Collect *all* materials. Collect all notes taken by you, the operators or other personnel. These may be valuable later if someone needs to research the source of a question or the cause of a technical difficulty. Another reason is that those notes may contain information that a competitor would love to have if the videoconference content was at all confidential. Do not toss them into a wastebasket, where any of the studio personnel or visitors can have access to them.

Congratulate your talent on a job well done (your planning and guidance will have ensured a fine job). Thank the crew members for their help.

Go home and relax. Tomorrow the final phase of the project begins.

SUMMARY

Only with careful planning can you effectively control your network on broadcast day. Take to the origination site all meeting details, including names and phone numbers of every vendor involved with the project. Be sure you have with you well-briefed assistants who can take care of secondary details such as caterers and audience seating. Above all, remain calm; many people will be looking to you to be their "rock," the one who can keep the whole process steady.

11

After the Event

The event is over. Accolades have been lavishly distributed. The talent has gone home. Now a new phase of work begins as you assess the success of the event, pay the bills and make plans for the videotape that resulted from your program.

TEN MINUTES AFTER THE EVENT

Two details will be of concern to you immediately after, but on the same day as, the event. The first is especially relevant if your event was a pay-per-view. That is getting an accurate audience and cash count.

For a pay-per-view, remember to instruct your meeting captains to remain at their sites following the close of the broadcast to call you with a final count of the total audience and a tally of the cash or credit card payments that resulted from walk-ins at the event. In this way you will know the same day how successful your event was from a financial standpoint. You have already kept tight control—through your signed vendor confirmation sheets—over costs. And since you will have undoubtedly had a system in place to count revenue through prepaid ticket sales, at the end of the day you will be able to do the simple calculation that will allow you to give a full and accurate financial report to your boss in the morning.

You will have avoided the problem that one videoconference manager had. She had allowed an outside vendor to handle everything, including all costs. As a result she had no idea where her organization stood following what appeared in audience size, to be a successful pay-per-view event. In fact, the vendor's record keeping was spotty. It was six weeks following the program before she discovered that they had *lost* money.

Simple controls could have made her job easier and her boss happier. She would have spotted before the event sites that could have been canceled due to low interest, possibly turning the event into a money-maker.

The second activity that should take place within a few minutes after the event is the completion of evaluation forms. This, of course, takes place at remote sites. You'll need to rely upon your meeting captains to see that evaluation forms (which came in a packet along with the facilitator's guide) are distributed, completed and returned. Ask the captains to return the forms immediately so that you can tabulate the results as soon as possible, while details of the event are still fresh in everyone's memory.

EVALUATING THE EVENT

There are three general ways in which to tell if an event was successful:

1. You may hear by word of mouth. If you get several sincere and enthusiastic calls from those who attended at remote sites, you'll know that the event was a success.
2. Check for quantifiable results. If your client's sales climb dramatically in the days and weeks immediately following your motivational sales videoconference, you will know you were a success.
3. Read the written evaluations. When you don't want to count on chance comments or you have no way to quantify the results as above, use an evaluation form.

Written Evaluations

Keep the form simple and brief. Immediately following the videoconference, the audience's minds will automatically turn to other matters. Catch them while the event is still a reality. Keep the form so easy to fill out and so convenient to turn in that it does not become a burden.

Be sensitive to the fact that some companies simply will not allow even their own personnel to be subjected to evaluations following an event, thinking that it is too much trouble.

Interestingly, companies that do believe in evaluating their events seem to derive a high level of satisfaction from their videoconferencing experiences. This could very well be due to the fact that, over time, their videoconferences get better and better because they take the results of their evaluations to heart.

EDS's Judy Masserang, who is heavily involved with General Motors' videoconference networks, says that Chevrolet, which has 38 sites (as of this writing) in its network, evaluates every videoconference it does. SmithKline Beckman and Procter & Gamble are also proponents of evaluations, taking the results quite seriously. The evaluation form used by both SmithKline and Procter & Gamble is included in the appendix.

Tabulating the Results

Once you have collected your evaluation forms, tabulate the results promptly. Write up a complete report, including both the good and bad feedback. Include especially pertinent comments that were made. Present the results to the people responsible for the event, those who produced it and those who paid for it, as soon as possible. If the evaluation uncovered shortcomings in the program, include ideas on how to avoid those problems the next time around. Ask others involved in the project to submit their ideas for improvement also. Keep in mind that the evaluation is meant as a useful feedback mechanism, not necessarily as a stamp of approval.

THE DAYS FOLLOWING THE VIDEOCONFERENCE

Q&A Follow-up

One idea used effectively by SmithKline Beckman is to distribute the questions and answers resulting from the videoconference, in print, to the attendees, and to those who should have attended but missed the event.

Include all the questions that were asked but not answered on air as well as a recap of those that were answered during the broadcast. This will reinforce the message of the videoconference and will allow all attendees to have a permanent record of information on a topic that may be quite important to them.

Paying the Bills

If the suggestions in this book have been followed regarding securing a firm contract from the production company and receiving written confirmation from meeting sites, downlinkers and audiovisual dealers, this part will be easy.

Easy is what you want it to be. Good record keeping will assure that when your event is done, it's done.

For ease of checking and payment, arrange all confirmation sheets in a logical order; alphabetical by vendor name is usually a safe choice. As the bills come in, check them against the confirmation sheets. When they agree, initial and date the invoice and pass it on for payment.

If the invoice and the confirmation sheet do not agree, find out why. Sometimes you will discover that a vendor had a legitimate need to add a piece of equipment at the last minute and deserves to be paid the additional sum. In other cases the vendor will have tacked on miscellaneous charges that were unordered and unneeded. In this case, pay only what has been agreed on in writing.

File copies of all paid invoices and supporting documentation, including names of contacts, phone numbers and information about the quality of service provided. This will come in handy and will save a great deal of work when you do your next videoconference.

MAKING USE OF YOUR VIDEOTAPE

It is recommended that every videoconference be videotaped at least for archival purposes. Beyond that, videoconference tapes have been used for productive purposes by several companies. Here is a sampling:

- Gerry Hendrixson at Procter & Gamble says that videotapes of their satellite events are distributed to those unable to attend the live program. Hendrixson also uses these tapes as demonstrations of the capabilities of videoconferencing for internal clients who are considering the technology.

- Judy Masserang of EDS says that she has seen bits and pieces of videoconferences show up as background footage in local Detroit news shows, evidently provided by General Motors and/or EDS public relations personnel.
- SmithKline Beckman has a closed circuit television system that is seen by all employees. Len Aulenbach has provided videoconference footage to be featured on their in-house TV news program.
- Dick Maresco of Associated Builders and Contractors likes to see his videoconferenced seminars make money. The resulting videotape is a serious part of his strategy. He says, "[You] must sell the teleconference as part of a whole training program. Send people [to the live event], buy the tape, spend months training on it." Maresco edits the resulting tapes into sections that are used later by members for roundtable discussions. The tapes range in price from $175 to $300. To help ensure overall profitability on a satellite-delivered seminar, Maresco arranges for the speaker to reduce the up—front fee in exchange for royalties on tape sales later.
- Caroline Laden, of the American Law Network, also creates an aftermarket for her videoconference tapes. They are edited and sold to lawyers and bar associations. The tapes generally sell for $150, and Laden says a real effort is made to have the edited tapes available within six weeks of the air date.

YOUR NEXT EVENT

Once your evaluations are in and tabulated, once the dust has settled, and as soon as others in your organization see how effective videoconferencing can be, you will probably be starting the process all over.

You will have learned a tremendous amount from your first effort. But there is always more to learn. Each event will take on a life of its own. Each one, regardless of how many you eventually do, will benefit from the management techniques you have learned in this book. Incorporate good planning and management into all your projects, and you will soon discover that any job—even a nationwide videoconference—is just a matter of performing one task after another in an orderly and well-managed succession.

SUMMARY

When the videoconference is finished, you will be anxious to wrap up the details and move on to your next project. Tight controls throughout the project will make this wrap-up easy. And the information that you will gain from your evaluations will make your next videoconference even better. With thought, you may also uncover uses for the resulting videotape that can earn dividends for your company either in cash or in public relations value.

Appendix A: Broadcast Checklist

PROGRAM TITLE_____

Program sponsor_____

   Contact_____   Phone_____

TECHNICAL REQUIREMENTS

Proposed day_____   Time_____

Broadcast origination location_____

Live transmission_____ Tape replay_____ Combination_____

Encrypted signal? [   ] Yes [   ] No

Broadcast data to be transmitted? [   ] Yes [   ] No

AUDIENCE

Fixed locations (identify audience size)_____

_____

_____

_____

Temporary receive locations (identify audience size)_____

_____

_____

_____

   Do temporary locations require audiovisual equipment rental?

      [   ] Yes   [   ] No   If yes, what?_____

Which time zones are involved?_____

   Compare to proposed broadcast time above.

Materials mailed to audience in advance of broadcast_____

Catering at receive sites (coffee/tea, soft drinks, food)?_____

PRODUCTION

Type of broadcast (press conference, training, executive message, new
   product introduction, motivational, etc.)

_____

Number of presenters_____

Type of presentations_____

Graphics (slides, transparencies, charts, PC)_____

   Monitors at origination site to view graphics?_____

What kind of set(s)? (podium, conference table, desk, etc.)_____

_____

Live audience at origination site?   [   ] Yes [   ] No Number_____
Question-and-answer (Q&A) session:
Live telephone_____
    Answered by telephone operators and written on 3 × 5 cards_____
    DEC Mail_____
    Questions from live audience_____
    Other_____
    Who will be answering questions?
        One person at podium_____
        Two people at podium_____
        Number of people at table_____ or in chairs_____
        Other_____
Broadcast data:
    Type of data (agenda, announcement, test)_____
    What type of terminal equipment do receive locations have?_____
    _____

Production company_____
    Contact_____   Phone_____

PRODUCTION ELEMENTS
    Number of cameras_____
    Character generator_____
    Teleprompter_____
    Slide chain_____
    Videotape inserts?   Format: ¾"_____   1"_____
    Videotape record?   Format: ¾"_____   1"_____
    Microphones: podium mic_____   lavalier mics_____
                          desk mics_____   wireless mic_____
                          mic for live audience questions_____
    Pre-production work (prepare open/close, taped inserts, slides,
        charts)_____
    Post-production work (editing, tape duplication)_____
    _____
    Setup time (day before, morning of)_____
    Strike time (same day, next day)_____
    Rehearsal time, if any_____
    Scripts_____
    Makeup_____
    Other:

Source: Courtesy of Judy Masserang, EDS Video Services.

Appendix B: Cost Justification Worksheet

PART A—RAW SALES COSTS—This is the amount you spend per day of sales calls. It's a starting point for examining the feasibility of a satellite-delivered call.

YOUR AVERAGE COST PER SALES CALL	$	_____
NUMBER OF CALLS EACH REP MAKES PER DAY	×	_____
COST OF ONE DAY OF SALES CALLS FOR EACH REP .	=	_____
NUMBER OF SALES REPS	×	_____
TOTAL COMPANY COST FOR ONE DAY OF SALES CALLS	=	_____

PART B—VALUE OF GROSS SALES VOLUME FOR ONE AVERAGE DAY—This is the amount your reps are *not* producing if they are out of the field for a meeting.

AVERAGE GROSS SALES PER YEAR PER REP	$	_____
NUMBER OF SELLING DAYS PER YEAR	%	_____
DAILY GROSS SALES VOLUME PER DAY PER REP	=	_____
NUMBER OF SALES REPS	×	_____
TOTAL GROSS SALES VOLUME PER DAY, ENTIRE COMPANY	=	_____

TOTAL FROM PART A	$ _____
TOTAL FROM PART B	$ _____

Appendix C: Service Confirmation Form

A/V and Downlink

Confirmation of downlinking or A/V equipment and services to be performed. Please review the following outline of services and equipment to be provided. Initial any changes; sign and return within _____ days to:

Mathis Consulting
PO Box 6959
Cincinnati, OH 45206

Company:_____

Address:_____

_____

Contact:_____Phone number: (_____)_____

After hours contact:_____

Phone number (after hours):_____

Event date:_____Day:_____

Times: Setup by_____Test starts:_____

Program starts_____

Program ends & teardown begins_____

Billing instructions: _____direct bill _____payment due prior

_____

Deliver to:_____Site contact:_____

Address:_____Phone number: (_____)_____

List of Equipment & Services   *Prices*

_____

_____

_____

_____

_____

	Subtotal:
	Tax:
	TOTAL:

I confirm that we will provide the services and equipment as outlined above except for changes submitted to us in writing. Additions/corrections are noted and initialed.

*Accepted by:*_____   _____

　　　　　　　　　　　　Name   Title

_____   _____

　　　　　　　　　　　Print name   Date

SIGN AND RETURN YELLOW COPY

Appendix D: Service Confirmation Form
Meeting Sites

Confirmation of meeting site services to be performed. Please review the following outline of services to be performed. Initial any changes; sign and return within _____ days to:
Mathis Consulting
PO Box 6959
Cincinnati, OH 45206

Receive site:_____

Address:_____

_____

Contact:_____ Phone number: (_____)_____

After hours contact:_____

Phone number (after hours) : (_____) _____

Event date:_____ Day:_____ Time:____

Title of event (to be posted):_____

Billing instructions:_____direct bill_____payment due prior

_____

_____

Setup:_____Max seating:_____

Room dimensions:_____ Ceiling height:_____

Obstructions:_____ Phone in room:_____

Description of event:_____

_____

Food arrangements:_____

_____

Additional breakout rooms:_____

Summary of charges:

Food/beverage:_____

Deposit:_____Deposit due:_____

Room rental:_____Phone in room:_____

Cancellation policy:_____

Additional arrangements:_____

_____

I confirm that we will perform the services as outlined above except for changes submitted to us in writing. Additions/corrections are noted and initialed.

Accepted by:_____   _____

                           Name   Title

_____   _____

           Print name   Date

SIGN AND RETURN YELLOW COPY

Appendix E: Site Facilitator's Guide

XYZ Corporation Satellite Network
XYZ National Satellite Sales Meeting
February 30, 1986

An XYZ Corporation national meeting will be held on February 30, 1986, live, by satellite, using a communications medium referred to as videoconferencing. The meeting will originate from the studios of WHYY television in Philadelphia. From that studio the program will be transmitted via a land-based microwave system to New York City, where it will be uplinked (transmitted) to a satellite orbiting the earth 22,300 miles above the equator.

The satellite to be used operates in the C-band, which is a frequency used by cable companies and most television networks. That satellite will amplify and retransmit the television signal to receive sites in 21 U.S. cities. These receive sites will be hotels where XYZ Corporation personnel will be gathered to watch the meeting and respond with questions by ordinary phone lines.

RESPONSIBILITIES OF SITE FACILITATORS

In the early hours of February 30, facilities will be set up for the videoconference. Upon arrival the site facilitator should check personally to be sure the following has been completed:

1. general session room set up classroom style
2. breakout rooms set up classroom style (exceptions requested by XYZ meeting captains are indicated on the attached detail sheet)
3. downlink dish installed outside the building
4. large-screen monitor cabled to the downlink and operating at the front of the room
5. backup projection unit on standby in case of technical problems
6. telephone installed and operational at the back of the general session room. This phone will be used during the system test for any contact you need to make with the origination site and

for the question-and-answer session. This phone will be hooked into the hotel switchboard, and you may need to access the hotel operator in the process of placing your calls.

Should any of the above not be completed by 9:00 a.m. *Eastern* time, contact the responsible technician or hotel employee. Their names are listed on the attached detail sheet.

INSTRUCTIONS FOR SYSTEM TEST

Do the following to test the system:

1. Arrive before the system test (11:00 a.m. Eastern, 10:00 a.m. Central, 9:00 a.m. Mountain, 8:00 a.m. Pacific).
2. Turn on monitor in general session room.
3. Check to be sure you can get an outside line on the phone in the general session room.
4. When instructed to do so by the monitor call 215/XXX-XXXX to confirm signal reception.
5. If no signal is being received after 15 minutes into the test, call 215/XXX-XXXX to report status.
6. Should there be continuing technical difficulties, please stand by to periodically update the origination site (215/XXX-XXXX) regarding progress.

IF SOMETHING GOES WRONG

Here are instructions to follow if there are problems:

1. With the hotel itself. If the meeting rooms are not set correctly, the room is too hot, the phone is not installed, etc., call the hotel contact whose name is listed on the attached sheet.
2. With the audiovisual equipment. The audiovisual technician (his name is on the attached sheet) is to remain on hand throughout the setup, test and complete event should help be needed. Call 215/XXX-XXXX if problem not resolved easily.
3. No picture or sound. Satellite technician (his name is on the attached sheet) will be on hand throughout the setup, test and complete event to correct. Call 215/XXX-XXXX to report the problem.

VIDEOCONFERENCE OUTLINE

11:00 a.m. Eastern Standard Time (10:00 Central, 9:00 Mountain, 8:00 Pacific). System test begins. The audiovisual and downlink technicians will have been on site well before the system test to install their equipment. You are to enter the general session room shortly before the test is to begin to take part in the test procedure.

11:00 a.m.–1:00 p.m. Eastern Standard Time. The test will go on air from the origination site in Philadelphia with a test signal comprised primarily of color bars and audio tone. Please be sure that your monitor is turned on and the sound turned up so that you are aware of the beginning of the test. A graphic will appear on the screen instructing you to call with your status. Call 215/XXX-XXXX to confirm that both picture and sound are being received. A phone to enable you to make this call and the calls during the question-and-answer session will be at the back of the general session room. During this system test please report any problems that you may perceive at your site.

At 12:30 p.m. the test signal will continue with a countdown. Graphics will appear on your screen informing you of the minutes remaining until the beginning of the videoconference.

PLEASE KEEP YOUR MONITOR ON—BOTH VIDEO AND AUDIO— AT ALL TIMES. SHOULD THERE BE A NEED TO SEND A MESSAGE TO ONE OR MORE SITES, IT WILL BE BROADCAST VIA THE SATEL-LITE NETWORK.

1:00 p.m. Eastern Standard Time (12:00 Central, 11:00 Mountain, 10:00 Pacific). The program will begin.

At approximately 2:00 p.m. Eastern Time a break will begin. That break is scheduled to last for 20 minutes. During that break you are to phone in your questions using the phone in the general session room. Call 215/XXX-XXXX to place questions. (Try again if you get a busy signal.)

QUESTION-AND-ANSWER PROCEDURE

Here are the procedures to follow:

- Take a stack of 3 × 5 index cards with you to the meeting for the use of attendees to write down their questions.
- The attendees should receive these cards before the program

begins so that they may write down their questions as they occur to them.

- At the break, collect the index cards. Read through the cards and eliminate duplicate questions. Note who has asked the question unless that person prefers to remain anonymous.
- Group your questions by topic category and relate them to each speaker's address.
- Call 215/XXX-XXXX to ask your questions. Your call will be answered by a fellow XYZ employee, who will write down the question and the name of the questioner (unless he or she prefers to remain anonymous).
- Your questions will be sorted, checked for redundancy, and then answered on the air during the one-hour Q&A session, which will follow the break.
- Please call often with questions and ask as many as you wish. Continue to call while the Q&A session is under way should those discussions spur other questions from your group.
- All questions and their answers will be published and mailed to you following the event. Questions that cannot be covered during the live Q&A will be answered in this manner.
- Please note that although there are 21 meeting sites in the network, just 10 telephone lines have been installed in Philadelphia to take your questions. This means that you will get a busy signal at some point. This also means that your questions should be delivered as succinctly as possible to give others in the network the opportunity to call.

YOU WILL BE INSTRUCTED VIA THE TELEVISION MONITOR REGARDING THE EXACT TIME TO BEGIN PHONING IN YOUR QUESTIONS.

At approximately 3:30 p.m. Eastern Standard Time, the videoconference is scheduled to end.

At the conclusion of the videoconference please complete the attached Evaluation Form and return it to:

XXXXXXXXXX XXXXXX, XXX.
P.O. Box XXXX
Cincinnati, OH XXXXX

A schedule of planned functions at your individual site is attached. Should you have questions regarding any of the arrangements please call us directly at 513/XXX-XXXX. Our office hours are 8:30 a.m. to 5:30

p.m. Eastern Time, Monday through Friday. Office hours will be extended to 8:00 p.m. for your convenience on February 28 and 29.

BILLING

Follow these procedures:

- Local XYZ Corporation personnel are responsible for their sleeping accommodations at time of checkout.
- All other charges are to be master-billed directly from the hotel to ABC Vendor, Inc.

Appendix F: Site Checklist

Meeting Details for Your Site

Hotel Site: Gaithersburg Marriott
620 Lake Forest Blvd.
Gaithersburg, MD 20877
301/XXX-XXXX

Contacts: XXXXXX XXXXXXX (sleeping accommodations)
XXX XXXXXXXX   (catering)

Sleeping Rooms: —Rooming lists to be sent directly from XYZ meeting captains
to hotel
—Attendees to pay for accommodations and related expenses
at checkout

ALL REMAINING FUNCTIONS TO BE BILLED THROUGH ABC VENDOR, INC.

Meeting Rooms:
February 30, 1986 . . . . . .General session room to seat 55 classroom

One breakout room to be open "U" with four seats
across the end and six on either side

Three breakout rooms to seat 17 each at four round
tables

Meals: PLEASE CALL YOUR HOTEL CONTACT BY FEBRUARY 25 WITH FINAL HEAD COUNT
FOR MEALS.

Final menu arrangements will be made the week of February 10. The following
general program is being ordered for your site. All meals, unless indicated otherwise, will be served for your group in a private room at the hotel.

All meals are to include some foods without dairy or citrus ingredients.

February 30, 1986 . . . . 7:00 a.m. Buffet breakfast to include
cereal and other choices

10:00 a.m. Coffee break w/tea, rolls
11:45 a.m. Lunch
 1:00 p.m. Videoconference begins
 3:45 p.m. Coffee break w/tea, soft
           drinks, fruit and cheese
 6:00 p.m. Cocktails
 7:00 p.m. Dinner

Audiovisual:

For videoconference . . . . Large-screen projection system w/ backup satellite receive dish

For remainder of meeting . . . . One flipchart easel and pad in each breakout room

One overhead projector, stand and screen in each breakout room

One 19″ TV monitor in each breakout room

Technician who will be at your site:

Projection equipment . . . . XXX XXXXXXXX
XXXXXXX Satellite Systems
703/XXX-XXXX

Satellite receive dish . . . . Same as above

PLEASE CALL ABC VENDOR, INC. AT 513/XXX-XXXX WITH CHANGES OR ADDITIONS TO THE ABOVE ARRANGEMENTS.

Appendix G: Evaluation Form

Site Facilitator: Please complete and mail to ABC Vendor, Inc., P.O. Box XXXX, Cincinnati, OH XXXXX.

1. This was the first videoconference I have ever attended.
   yes   no

2. I would like to hold other meetings using a videoconference.
   1   2   3   4   5
   Strongly Disagree   Strongly Agree

3. The picture quality was good.
   1   2   3   4   5
   Strongly Disagree   Strongly Agree

4. The audio quality was good.
   1   2   3   4   5
   Strongly Disagree   Strongly Agree

5. The technicians were helpful.
   1   2   3   4   5
   Strongly Disagree   Strongly Agree

6. The technicians were courteous.
   1   2   3   4   5
   Strongly Disagree   Strongly Agree

7. The hotel staff was easy to work with.
   1   2   3   4   5
   Strongly Disagree   Strongly Agree

8. The program was well produced.
   1   2   3   4   5
   Strongly Disagree   Strongly Agree

9. Enough time was allowed for answering questions.

1	2	3	4	5
Strongly Disagree				Strongly Agree

10. I liked the hotel where the meeting was held.

1	2	3	4	5
Strongly Disagree				Strongly Agree

11. Site where you attended: Hotel name_____
                                                City_____

12. What did you like best about the videoconference?

13. What did you like least about the videoconference?

14. Comments:

Bibliography

Buyer's Guide. Altadena, CA: TeleSpan Publishing Corporation, yearly.

Downlink Directory. Littleton, CO: Virginia A. Ostendorf, Inc., 1985.

E–ITV (Educational and Industrial Television). New York, NY: Broadband Information Services, Inc., monthly.

Floyd, Steve, and Beth Floyd. *Handbook of Interactive Video*. White Plains, NY: Knowledge Industry Publications, Inc., 1982.

Hotel & Travel Index. New York, NY: Murdoch Magazines Business Publications Division, quarterly.

Lazer, Ellen A., Martin C. J. Elton, James W. Johnson, et al. *The Teleconferencing Handbook*. White Plains, NY: Knowledge Industry Publications, Inc., 1983.

NAVA/ICIA Membership Directory. Fairfax, VA: International Communications Industries Association, yearly.

Official Meeting Facilities Guide. New York, NY: Murdoch Magazines Business Publications Division, semi-annual.

The Satellite Directory. Potomac, MD: Phillips Publishing, Inc., yearly.

Teleconferencing Directory. Madison, WI: Center for Interactive Programs, University of Wisconsin-Extension, yearly.

Teleconferencing Resources Directory. White Plains, NY: Knowledge Industry Publications, Inc., 1986.

The TeleSpan Newsletter. Altadena, CA: TeleSpan, monthly.

Uplink Directory. Littleton, Co: Virginia A. Ostendorf, Inc., 1986.

Utz, Peter. *The Video User's Handbook*. White Plains, NY: Knowledge Industry Publications, Inc., 1982.

Video Manager. White Plains, NY: Knowledge Industry Publications, Inc., monthly.

Video Register and Teleconferencing Resources Directory. White Plains, NY: Knowledge Industry Publications, Inc., yearly.

Wiegand, Ingrid. *Professional Video Production.* White Plains, NY: Knowledge Industry Publications, Inc., 1985.

INDEX

ABC, 81
American Bar Association, 22
American Home Sewing
    Association, 21
American Law Institute, 22
American Law Network, 33,
    34, 38, 94, 100, 139
Applications
  corporate users, 18-21
  fund-raising, 22-23
  pay-per-view, 21-22
  speaker delivery, 22
Associated Builders and
    Contractors, 22, 33, 139
Association of Hospital
    Television Networks, 108
AT&T, 5
Aulenbach, Len, 12, 48, 53,
    58, 122, 139

Bonneville, 5, 80
Briscoe, Keith, 22
Buena Vista College, 22

Caldwell, Phillip, 19
C-band, 81
  See also Networking
CBS, 81
Chancellor, John, 23
Chrysler, 19, 68
Communications Satellite
    Corp. (COMSAT), 7
ConferSat, 107
Costs
  budgeting, 25-27
  comparison w/other

methods, 27-29
  funding of, 32-35
  justification of, 29-32

Donahue, Phil, 60

Electronic Data Systems
    (EDS) Corp., 19, 23, 38,
    61, 88, 95, 121, 137, 139
ESPN, 81, 82

Federal Communications
    Commission (FCC), 5
Ferguson, Lee, 38, 53, 66, 75,
    76
Ford, 19
Fortune 500, 18

General Motors, 8, 19-20, 23,
    38, 137, 139

HBO, 81, 82
Hendrixson, Gerry, 11-12, 41,
    42, 68, 138-139
Hewlett-Packard, 8, 10
Holiday Inn, Inc., 8, 102

Iacocca, Lee, 14
International Telecommuni-
    cations Satellite
    Organization
    (INTELSAT), 7
Irwin Communications, 9
Irwin, Susan J., 9-10

J.C. Penney, 8

Kiam, Victor, 14
Knight, Kip, 12-14, 27-28, 53, 54, 61
Ku-band, 81-82
    See also Networking

Laden, Caroline, 33, 34, 38, 94-95, 99, 100, 139

Mann, Clarence, 37, 50-51, 54, 60, 61, 62-63, 74, 75, 76, 77, 121, 122
Maresco, Dick, 21, 22, 33, 34, 139
Marriott Corp., 102
Masserang, Judy, 19, 23, 38, 54, 61, 75, 88, 95, 99, 121-122, 137, 139
Mechanical Contractors Association of America, 21
Meeting Planners International, 109
Meeting sites,
  and site captains, 110-111
  and site facilitator's guide, 111-112
  space requirements for, 109-110
  types of, 100-109
Merrill Lynch, 8
MicroAge, 9
Murphy, Thomas, 23

National Dairy Council, 21
National University of Teleconferencing Network (NUTN), 105
NAVA/ICIA Membership Directory, 91

NBC, 23, 81
Networking, 8
  and technicians, 88-89
  audiovisual equipment 91-94
  checklist, 96-97
  downlinks, 3, 85-88, 89-91
  sample budget, 95
  satellite choice, 80-82
  scrambling, 94-95
  uplinks, 3, 82-85

Ostendorf, Virginia, 84, 88

PBS, 81, 107
Planning and Preparation
  first meeting, 38-42
  problems, 45
  second meeting, 42-45
Post, Telephone and Telegraph (PTT), 7
Private Satellite Network, 10
Procter & Gamble, 11-12, 20-21, 27, 37, 38, 41, 53, 54, 57, 61, 66, 67, 68, 74, 75, 105, 137, 138
Production process
  pre-production, 47-64
  rehearsal to on-air, 65-77
Project management, 113-120
  after the event, 135-140
  day of event, 121-134
Public Service Satellite Consortium, 18

RCA, 5

Satellease, 88
Satellite Business Systems, 5
The Satellite Directory, 7

Sat Time, 80
Sears Roebuck & Co., 8
Smith Kline and French
   Laboratories, 12, 21
   See also SmithKline
   Beckman
SmithKline Beckman, 21, 37,
   48, 53, 67, 122, 137, 139
   See also Smith Kline and
   French Laboratories
Star Wars, 60

Texas Instruments, 10, 22
Transmission
   domestic, 5-8
   international, 5-8
   satellite, 3-4

University Illinois, 23

University Wisconsin,
   Madison, 18
Uplink Directory, 84, 88

Videoconferencing
   definition, 1-2
   when to use, 8-14
Video Register and
   Teleconferencing
   Resources Directory, 5, 7
Video Star, 5, 88
VideoStar Connections, 10
Viscom International, 7
Voluntary Hospitals of
   America, 108

Western Union, 5
World, 5, 80

About the Author

Georgia Mathis has worked in hi-tech communications for over 15 years. She founded Cincinnati Uplink, Inc. in 1983. In her role as president she consults with clients on videoconferencing and oversees the management of turnkey videoconference projects. Her clients have included Procter & Gamble, Smith Kline & French Laboratories and General Electric.

Mathis has a master's degree in journalism/public relations from the W. Page Pitt School of Journalism at Marshall University. Her background includes six years with IBM (whose project management techniques she brings to the videoconferencing arena). She has also acted as Director, Satellite Communications for WCET-TV.

Mathis is the author of several articles on videoconferencing and executive presentation skills.